WICCA FOR BEGINNERS

THE ULTIMATE GUIDE TO WICCAN MAGIC, TRADITIONS, RITUALS, AND DEITIES. HOW TO FOLLOW THE WITCHCRAFT PATH FOR THE SOLITARY PRACTITIONER.

Table of contents

Chapter 1: Introduction to Wicca

Chapter 2: Wiccan Beliefs - The Craft

Chapter 3: Wiccan Morality

Chapter 4: Wiccan Rituals

Chapter 5: The Wiccan Ritual & Magic

Chapter 6: The Wiccan Book of Shadows

Chapter 7: First Steps for A Novice-How to Start on Your Personal Wiccan Path

Chapter 8: Solitary Practice VS Covens

Conclusion

Chapter 1: Introduction to Wicca

What is Wicca? In the broadest sense, Wicca, also known as The Craft, is a term used to encompass most forms of modern Pagan Witchcraft. Many people don't know what it means to be Wiccan, or who a witch might be today. In the past, throughout history, witches have been persecuted for being agents of evil, or even Devil worshippers. While Wiccans certainly aren't perfect, as are none of us, they are no more evil than any other group of people with the same spiritual views. For Wicca itself is not the practice of Satanic worship nor Devil worship, Wicca is, in essence, the exact opposite to this and has nothing to do with the Dark Arts, unlike these stereotyped folklores. The religion of Wicca, as we will soon discover, promotes a profound respect for nature, and the desire to achieve harmony within the natural world. This connection and unity to the natural order come through openings one's self to the ways of truth and love. Thus, coming into alignment with the elements, or our natural state of being, to continue to evolve emotionally, physically and spiritually as a collective.

To many people's surprise Wiccans encompass a broad spectrum of people as well. A Wiccan could be a typical businessman, that performs rituals every week as a high priest in his coven, or that nice older lady who lives down the block, and always used to send you cookies when she heard you were feeling down (You had no idea she was giving you healing energies, too!). Wiccans are doctors, and handymen, housewives and rock stars. Wicca is a way of life that many people share, and a community of giving and acceptance worldwide. Wiccans are those who share and practice these beliefs and ideals. Yet the religion has no recognition of hierarchy, leadership or sectarianism. The beauty of Wicca as a belief system is that it is not limited to one religion or one ideal, yet open to all systems of beliefs as an adaptation to your way of living, to enhance your current belief system. In a narrower definition, Wicca is a religion developed and descended from British Traditional Wicca (BTW), or Witchcraft. It's core practices and rituals, have come together over time throughout history. Yet it was not until the early 19th Century that this world was bought to the public attention after centuries of being stigmatized.

Many people refer to Gerald Gardener, also known as Scire, to be the father of Wicca. Due to his original development and culmination of these ancient practices throughout the 1940s and 1950s that Gardner and later with collaboration by Doreen Valiente, into what is known today as Wicca. These two spiritual pioneers outlined and developed what would later come to be known as part of today's British Traditional Wicca, drawing on a wide, and sometimes highly disputed set of ancient Pagan and Hermetic belief systems. This included but never limited to tapping into Freemasonry, Druidism, Shamanic work, modern science and medicine, calling upon works of the likes of Aleister Crowley. Other spiritual leaders in the Wiccan and Pagan community would leave their indelible marks on the rich, varied and sometimes misunderstood spiritual faith called Wicca. From fierce opposition in the form of scathing British scorn to the New Age boom of Neo-Pagan and Wiccan theologies of the 1960s counterculture in the U.S.A. Two recent poles into American Religious Identification identify Wicca as one the fastest growing, evolving and ever-changing spiritual choice for millions of people.

The term Wicca itself is often disputed, yet has the roots to Anglo-Saxon language, meaning "wise one" this later was adopted in the Old English language to form term "witch," the term that many people have known practitioners of Wicca by for the last centuries. This original term was readopted due to the exploration into the ways of old and as a memoir back to the roots of Wicca's as a polytheistic belief system, as the word which was chosen by the Old British English and given a reputation for the Dark Arts throughout the Early Christian Era. Today, those who call themselves Wiccan are practitioners of a widely varied and diverse tradition, based in British Traditional Wicca, but encompassing many different offshoots and beliefs.

Wicca's Origins

Gerald Gardner was an amateur anthropologist and archaeologist, as well as a British author of titles such as *High Magic's Aid* (1949), a fictional account based in Medieval England. Due to Witchcraft laws still being extremely harsh even at that time in England, Gardner had to fictionalize his account of Wicca. He also claimed that there were requirements of secrecy placed upon him by those who taught him his Craft. *Witchcraft Today* (1951), and *Meaning of Witchcraft* (1959), both later, non-fiction accounts of his views and evolving insights into Wicca that brought the little know spiritual faith to worldwide attention. He was a pioneer of Wicca as we know it today, and one of its most controversial figures to date. However, as many Wiccans know, even with being heralded as the "Father of Wicca" Gardner, was not the first Wicca, but is giving this title as being at the forefront of exposing an ancient practice to the public eye. Gardner, also known by the craft name Scire, was the founding father of the Bricket Wood coven in the 1940s, through which he was intent on bringing Wicca to the public's attention. Commonly referred to as the Father of Wicca, Gardner's initiates would go on to help spread Wicca, it's traditions, branches and offshoots throughout the U.K, Australia, and North America. Gardner was heavily criticized for publicity-seeking, false claims about source material from which he drew his religious and educational backgrounds, as well as some of his personal habits and his association with the teachings of Aleister Crowley which many thought to be Satanist influences. He remains a key figure in the history of Wicca as we know it today.

September of 1939 saw Gardener initiated into the New Forest coven, a self-proclaimed "witch cult" that practiced what they referred to as simply a "pre-Christian, pagan religion". The New Forest coven was allegedly also part of "Operation Cone of Power", a gathering of witches during 1940, in which members raised a magical cone of power in order to energetically stop Nazi Germany from invading Great Britain. Gardner later went on to form his own coven in the 1940s, with his wife Donna, calling it Bricket Wood coven and adding elements of Freemasonry, Druidic and Hermetic teachings, as well as the writings of Aleister Crowley to the New Forest coven's doctrines. He later initiated Doreen Valiente, as well as several other forerunners of Wiccan history, and collaborated with her to create the Gardnerian Book of Shadows, the original model from which many grimoires are formed.

Doreen Valiente was a British poet and prolific author of Wiccan and Pagan literature. Some of her books include *Where Witchcraft Lives* (1962), *An ABC of Witchcraft* (1973), *Natural Magic* (1975), *Witchcraft for Tomorrow* (1978), *The Rebirth of Witchcraft* (1979), *Charge of the Goddess*(2000), and *Doreen Valiente - Witch*(2016). She also co-authored Gerald Gardner's Book of Shadows, and Witchcraft-A Tradition Renewed with Evan John Jones, Second Magister of the Clan of Tubal Cain. Valiente began practicing magic as a teenager and was initiated into the Gardnerian tradition in 1953, aged 31. Quickly becoming High Priestess of the Bricket Wood coven, she contributed heavily to the original Gardnerian Book of Shadows, removing much of the material Gardner had taken from the teachings of Aleister Crowley, seeing it as possibly damaging to public opinion. After leaving the Bricket Wood coven in 1957, due to disputes about the authenticity of Gardner's claims as well as increasing tensions between the two (although later she would reconcile with Gardner and remain friends with him until his death), she went on to form her own coven for a brief time, before going on to work with numerous leaders prominent in the Wiccan and Pagan communities, including Robert Cochrane, Raymond Howard, as well as Stuart and Janet Farrar, also joining some of their covens as well. Valiente is credited with being the Mother of Modern Wicca, and through her works and books, as having a hand in the expansion and early development of Wicca.

Robert Cochrane, born Roy Bowers, founded the Tradition known as Cochrane's Craft in the 1960s. While not identifying as a Wiccan himself, Cochrane coined the term "Gardnerian" as an insult to and directed a great deal of animosity towards Gerald Gardner and his followers. Bowers developed a very similar version of witchcraft and spiritual tradition, when he formed his coven that would later become the basis for his Clan of Tubal Cain, taking the name from the First Hebrew smith. While Cochranianism holds some similarities to Gardnerian Wicca, Cochrane took a much more relaxed and naturalistic stance on ritual and worship. Thus, paving the way for a new form of Wicca to take place and be born into the modern traditional practice. Several of Cochrane's letters have been published in which he speaks openly about his views, spiritual traditions and opinions on both Gardnerianism, and his Craft, although Cochrane never authored any full books. Cochrane disagreed with many of Gardner's tenets and spoke out against Gardner and his Tradition. This branch of Witchcraft uses no Book of Shadows and follows a different Horned God as it's male duality. Its practitioners wear robes of black during rituals and use slightly different magical tools and terminology. Considered a gifted ritualist and an often-forgotten forerunner to Wicca as we know it today, Cochrane encouraged many Wiccans to step out of what they felt were the overly constricting philosophies of Gardnerianism, and adhere to what he termed the Old Witch Law, instead of the Wiccan Rede, which states:

Do not do what you desire - do what is necessary.
Take all you are given - give all of yourself.
What I have - - - I hold!
When all else is lost, and not until then, prepare to die with dignity.

Robert Cochrane, in a letter written to Joe Wilson

By the late 1980s, Wicca had expanded and given rise to numerous, divergent traditions. Many of these included groups and covens completely independent of Gardner's original Tradition, including Dianic Wicca, founded by Alexander Sanders, and also giving rise to other Pagan and Neo-Pagan spiritualities, including The Goddess movement, Reconstructionism, Heathenry, and Neo-Druidism.

Chapter 2: Wiccan Beliefs - The Craft

It is easiest to describe the most widely used divinities within the Wiccan system as those of a ditheistic system comprised of the All-Father and All-Mother. These two are known by many other names, including the Sky-Father and Earth Mother, as well as The Horned God and the Mother Goddess terms used most often in Wicca. Carrying over into most Wiccan beliefs is that these two Divinities represent the best, most virtuous ideologies that men and women should strive for in their own lives. This duality is representative not only of human traits yet can be found in all of life, this eternal balance.

Deities

The Horned God also referred to as the Lord, represents the male aspects of the Wiccan belief system and the masculine energy within the universe. He is the Protector, associated with the forest and the sun, virility and the Wild Hunt during Imbolc celebrations. The Lord is the embodiment of the wilderness, the energetic forces of animals and wild places. Often represented as being horned, or having antlers, symbolizing his duality as Creator and Destroyer. The Horned God is also often depicted as having a '"Three-fold nature", due to having the three aspects of Youth or Warrior, Father, and Sage that mirror a man's journey through life on a Divine Energetic level.

The Lady, also known as Diana, Aradia, Hecate is the balanced counterpart of the Horned God. Mother-Goddess, as she is also called, is also associated with Freya and the Norns from Norse Mythology. She embodies the archetypes of Maiden, Mother, and Crone, and personifies not only a woman's Life Journey but also the phases of the Moon, the sea and the stars. She is the embodiment of the female energy within the universe. Aspects of the Mother Goddess include fertility, Nature, rebirth, cycles, nurturing, healing and wisdom.

While The Horned God and The Goddess are two of the most widely revered deities in Wicca, they are by no means the only ones. While some Wiccans accept the concept of Polytheism, believing in the existence of many Gods/Goddesses, still others venerate only one Deity, whether it be a version of the Mother Goddess, a single all-powerful, multi-faceted Creator, or even a Universal Consciousness. Still, others view the gods as "Archetypes" or constructs, concepts created by humans to define the forces in the world around them, to be used as a focal point for the Will. No matter one's beliefs monotheistic or polytheistic, Wicca, at its heart is an inclusive, life-affirming, spiritual view. One that urges its practitioners to maintain on a positive outlook toward destructive forces in the world around them, as it is this balance between life and death that simultaneously promotes a healthy, balanced relationship with Nature and the Cosmos. You will want to take time to find out which Divinities call to you, or those you "resonate" best with, be they the Triple Goddess, Ra, Diana, or The Dagda. Learn what rituals and ceremonies you connect with and try some out on your own. Wicca is a very individualistic unique Spiritual practice, meaning what works for one person, won't necessarily be right for someone else. The only way to find out what works best for you is to take the knowledge you find, and try and put it into practice. This will allow you to find the Wiccan path that gives you the most spiritual fulfilment.

The Afterlife

Wicca has no real, "set in stone" views on the afterlife. While many Wiccans share the same set of core beliefs, they generally came to their conclusions through study, research and Life experience. Wiccans usually try to focus more on celebrating a life lived well, rather than mourning a death. In fact, many Wiccans mourn only for those who are "left behind", the friends and loved ones of those who have passed on, for their loss. A great many Wiccans believe in some form of re-incarnation, be it linear, familial, or more akin to the Buddhist doctrines. Others hold fast to the idea of The Summerland, a higher plane of existence, similar in nature and concept to The Elysian Fields of Greek mythology, or the Happy Hunting Grounds of the Lakota people of North America. Still, others believe that when we die, we return to a Divine Source made up of all the spirits of those who came before, and is also where we get our spirit when we are born. Some Wiccans believe that nothing happens after a person dies, and we, along with our spirit and energies simply cease to exist. Very often it is simply accepted that a person will experience the afterlife of the Divinities they most work and identify with.

As mentioned before, Wiccans generally, try to celebrate Life, and whether a witch is bound for Valhalla, Cerridwen's Cauldron or the Summerlands is completely the choice of the individual practitioner. Wicca is a spiritual path toward knowledge and understanding, and it is still growing and evolving today. Just as an individual's views can easily change as we learn, grow, and experience Life, as Wiccans, this change is accepted as part of a natural cycle of birth, growth, death and rebirth. Those who practice Wicca are typically open-minded, tolerant, and acceptant of differing spiritual beliefs, seeing these differences as opportunities for knowledge, enlightenment, and a better understanding of their fellow human beings.

Nature and Wicca

Nature stands at the very heart of the Wiccan tradition, and is vitally important in the practice of Witchcraft, or "The Craft". One of Wicca's core beliefs is that a person should live in harmony with Nature, and balance the Elements within themselves. Magic itself draws its energy from the Five Elements (Air, Fire, Water, Earth and Spirit), and Nature is the physical embodiment of those forces. When a witch draws upon the Elements, they are calling on them to provide them with the power to reach their goals, be they healing, divination, or changes in their personal life. But this can only happen if the Wiccan is in tune with Nature and balanced in their energies. Magic is widely practiced in natural settings, this is because the elemental forces that create magic are part of Nature, and by being close to those forces, we can better manipulate them to manifest the will.

Most Wiccans are in tune with the seasons, the harvest cycles, phases of the moon, and the passing of the Sabbats. The Wiccan Sabbats are sacred Holy days, that celebrate the changing of the seasons, the Horned God, his role as the Virile Father who gives His seed to the Mother Goddess, as well as the planting and harvest cycles. The Earth's cycles of growth are important to a Wiccan to know what to harvest and when to plant. Esbats are celebration rituals for the phases of the moon. Celebrating and honoring its connections with the Mother-Goddess in her aspects of Maiden-Mother-Crone, a cycle life to which all women submit. This cycle corresponds to the waxing and waning of the moon and is celebrated as a part of the growth cycle of all life. This gives Wiccans a very centered viewpoint of the world around them, knowing that we are connected to nature and the forces that embody it.

Many Wiccans meditate out of doors, to be better attune themselves with nature to achieve inner peace, balance, and to focus willpower. This close association with nature means that Wiccans understand that because all life is interconnected, further attunement with nature will lead to spiritual insight, growth, and enlightenment. Many Wiccans are constantly involved with the environment because they know that in taking care of the earth, it will take care of us. A great many Wiccans practice Herbalism and have an extensive knowledge of healing plants, where to find them, and how to use them in spells, rituals, and everyday life. Gardens and forests are special for Wiccan practitioners because these places of growth are where nature is most abundant, and "visible" through the existence of the cycles of life, death and rebirth. Hedge witches not only grow their gardens but also spend much of their time out in the forests and woods, mountains or fields communing with nature, as well as astral journeying in order to be able to speak with the spirits of nature itself, such as plants and animals. They are renowned to invest long hours out in the wild places, studying all the mysteries that the outdoors and Mother Earth will teach them.

The Core Traditions of Wicca/Witchcraft

Since the 1940s, Wicca has been growing and evolving as a spiritual choice for people all over the world. The reason for this may be the acceptance and adaptability of its core principles. People are often attracted to Wicca because there are so many different traditions, with no authoritative hierarchy, overall standardizations or rigid dogmas. From its stepping into the public eye through the Bricket Wood coven, and still today, Wicca has always been a mutable, flexible and an inclusive spiritual devotion. Because of this, it is impossible to narrow Wicca itself down to just one specific theological structure, or concept. Wiccans base their spirituality around the deeper understanding of the natural order. With the belief that every person has the capacity of good and evil within them. There are many spiritual ideologies that are classified as Wiccan, so let us take a moment to explore some of the more well-known:

- Gardnerian Wicca is the original "coven" of modern-day Wicca. Developed by Gerald Gardner in the U.K. This branch of Wicca has a very secretive doctrine and can be difficult to learn about if not an initiate of one of its covens. In Gardnerian Wicca, one can only be initiated into Wicca by another Gardnerian witch. This means that every "true Gardnerian" can trace their roots back to Gardner's original coven, called Bricket Wood. Covens in this branch of Wicca traditionally have thirteen members and use Gerald Gardner's original Book of Shadows, passed down from him to his initiates, who in turn passed it to theirs. Rituals are often highly elaborate, and some of the most devout members of this traditional practice ritual nudity, as well as "The Great Rite".

The Great Rite is an act of ritual intercourse, performed during a ceremony by the High Priestess or High Priest to call upon the energy of The God or Goddess respectively, to attain states of spiritual awareness and revelation. This is often now done symbolically with an Athame or Wand and Chalice or Cauldron. Gardnerian Wicca also applies three degrees of initiation, which all initiates must pass before starting their own coven.

- Cochrane's Craft, also known as Cochranianism, was started in 1951 by English witch Robert Cochrane. Naming his coven, The Clan of Tubal Cain after the first blacksmith, Cochrane developed a system of Wicca completely independent of Gardnerian Wicca, and with some notable differences. Instead of The Wiccan Rede, and Three-fold Law, adherents of Cochran's Craft followed what he termed the "Old Witch Law". They were also known to perform rituals wearing robes, instead of "skyclad", or nude, did not make use of a Book of Shadows, and used a forked staff, called a stang, as a sort of moveable altar. Cochrane's disuse of a Book of Shadows may have given his rituals a more relaxed feel, leaving his followers free to pursue their own spirituality openly.

- Alexandrian Wicca takes its name partly from one of its founders, Alex Sanders, and also from the Great Library of Alexandria. Alex Sanders and his wife, Maxine, founded this branch of Wicca but were originally members of the Gardnerian Tradition. A key difference between the two Traditions is the Alexandrian Wiccan's incorporation of and placing more significance on the archetypes of the Oak and Holly Kings as aspects of the Horned God. Members are also much more relaxed in their attitudes of nudity, in that they choose whether they wish to practice their faith fully clothed, or not. There is also a greater degree of malleability and acceptance towards members finding their path to personal growth.

- Celtic and Druidic Wicca are technically two different offshoots of Wicca, but practicing members often meld aspects of both branches into their practices. Celtic Wicca takes many of its practices from the ancient Celts, mainly the Irish, Welsh, Cornish and Gaul's, and so takes its deities and Sabbat names from these pantheons and histories. The Celtic branch of Wicca also traditionally uses the Ogham (an ancient Gaelic writing system, similar in concept to Norse runes) for divination and magical symbolism, and some practitioners of this offshoot also use the Celtic classification of three Elements, namely Earth, Sky, and Water.

- Druidic Wicca has more of a shamanistic, nature-based spiritual view than that found in other traditional branches of Wicca. Practitioners of Druidic Wicca place more reverence in herbal magics, stone and crystal workings, and animals in their Ethos, particularly ravens, stags and boars. Druidic Wicca places more belief in animal spirits and the elements of nature, than traditional Wiccan deities, and finds its roots in pre-Christian England and Ireland.

- Seax-Wica is based in the traditions of the Anglo-Saxon peoples of the fifth to eleventh centuries and shares many similarities with Norse Wicca. Seax-Wica honors the deities of Wodan, Thunor, Frig or Freya and Tiw. The lineage also emphasises the use on the Norse Runes. Founded in 1973 by Raymond Buckland, a British born Wiccan who came to the U.S. in 1962. Buckland was initiated into the Gardnerian Tradition in 1963, after returning to England for the ceremony. He then published *The Tree* in 1974 and later taught Seax-Wica through a correspondence course. His intention in publishing *The Tree* was to allow those who wanted to become Wiccans, through means self-initiation or even consecrate their own sacred magical tools, could be a part of the Wiccan faith without the need to be initiated by an existing coven. Seax-Wica covens also differ from Gardnerian Wicca in that its covens are more of a democracy, with the Priestess' and Priests being voted on, and serving out terms. This branch does not normally use a Book of Shadows at all, making the path more readily available for the novice since members do not take oaths of secrecy, like more traditional Wiccans. An added emphasis on Herbalism and divination are also hallmarks of Seax-Wicca. Many traditional Gardnerians can trace their lineage back through Buckland, who formed The New York coven when he arrived in the U.S. which remained in practice until his divorce when both he and his wife left the coven.

- Norse Wicca is steeped in the traditions and cosmology of the pre-Christian, Scandinavian peoples. With many of the same values of Seax-Wica, including a reverence nature, both share the same, or similar pantheons, deities, and the use of Norse runes for divination, with similar views of the afterlife. Many of Norse Wicca's tenets also follow along the same spiritual veins as Wicca itself, including similar moralistic leanings. However, unlike Wicca, they also go on to recognize more than just the usual Wiccan Female and Male ditheistic system. Many Norse Wiccans are solitary practitioners, with few covens. Practitioners of Norse Wicca blend The Long Rede and the Law of Three with teachings from the Poetic Eddas as not only their moralistic guide, but also for rituals, and Sabbats, because of slightly differing calendars. Norse Wicca is not as widely accepted as many other traditions of Wicca, this being because of an unfortunate (and wrong) animosity from many other Pagan groups and individuals that insist Norse Wicca is an impossible mixture and the two spiritualities that cannot possibly be cohesively bound together, but practitioners of Norse Wicca will tell you that while some of the methods may differ greatly, the two cultures were very spiritually similar, placing value on living a virtuous life, honoring the Divinities, and manifesting our own destiny through the will.

- Created by Zsuzsanna Budapest, Dianic Wicca originated in the United States through the 1970s and is a strictly feministic tradition, in that it focuses solely on the Goddess in all Her aspects and de-emphasizes the polarities of gender, like more traditional Gardnerian or Alexandrian Wicca. Because the Dianic practice focuses largely on the feminine the supremacy of the Mother Goddess, this branch of Wicca is often more keenly aware of political and societal issues faced by women, often having rituals exclusively tailored for healing such trauma as rape and spousal abuse. Dianic Wicca can be gender exclusive, in that some practicing covens do not admit men into practice, and some will admit lesbian and bi-sexual females but no one else from the LGBTQ community.

- Eclectic Wiccans blend their own version of Wicca by drawing on one or more theologies or metaphysical orientations and may even add original rituals and practices of their own, as well as their views on deities and gods. Eclectic Wicca is the most widely practiced form of Wicca today, being much more accessible, and less formalized than most traditional branches of Wicca.

Chapter 3: Wiccan Morality

The Wiccan Rede is a series of instructions and advice given in poetic form, that sums up the core of Wiccan morality, sort of an "ethical code of conduct". The short form simply says: "*And it Harm none, do what ye will.*", meaning people (Wiccans) are free to pursue their own goals, aspirations, and fulfill their own will, as long as no one is harmed by their actions (this includes the individual's physical, emotional and spiritual well-being, as well). The original poem, known as The Long Rede, expands upon this, advising on various topics from spell casting and Holy days in the Wiccan tradition, to nature lore, herb craft, and emotional advice.

Rede of the Wicca

Bide the Wiccan Laws ye must In Perfect Love and Perfect Trust.
Live an' let live - Fairly take an' fairly give.
Cast the Circle thrice about To keep all evil spirits out.
To bind the spell every time - Let the spell be spake in rhyme.
Soft of eye an' light of touch - Speak little, listen much.
Deosil go by the waxing Moon - Sing and dance the Wiccan rune.
Widdershins go when the Moon doth wane, An' the Werewolf howls by the dread Wolfsbane.
When the Lady's Moon is new, Kiss thy hand to Her times two.
When the Moon rides at Her peak Then your heart's desire seek.
Heed the Northwind's mighty gale - Lock the door and drop the sail.
When the wind comes from the South, Love will kiss thee on the mouth.
When the wind blows from the East, Expect the new and set the feast.

When the West wind blows o'er thee, Departed spirits restless be.
Nine woods in the Cauldron go - Burn them quick an' burn them slow.
Elder be ye Lady's tree - Burn it not or cursed ye'll be.
When the Wheel begins to turn - Let the Beltane fires burn.
When the Wheel has turned a Yule, Light the Log an' let Pan rule.
Heed ye flower bush an' tree - By the Lady Blessèd Be.
Where the rippling waters go Cast a stone an' truth ye'll know.
When ye have need, Hearken not to others greed.
With the fool no season spend Or be counted as his friend.
Merry meet an' merry part - Bright the cheeks an' warm the heart.
Mind the Threefold Law ye should - Three times bad an' three times good.
When misfortune is enow, Wear the Blue Star on thy brow.
True in love ever be Unless thy lover's false to thee.
Eight words ye Wiccan Rede fulfill - An' it harm none, Do what ye will.

Gwen Porter- The Green Egg, 1975

In 1973 the American Council of Witches was assembled by Carl Llewellyn Weschcke, who was president of Llewellyn Worldwide Ltd, a large publisher of New Age and Occult books, based in Woodbury, Minnesota. The members were an independent group of Pagans, NeoPagans, and Wiccans. All unified with the one goal, bring unity to the many diverse Spiritual Paths of Wicca, Paganism, and NeoPaganism, and to bring clarity to a great many misconceptions surrounding the Pagan and Wiccan communities. They also wanted to remain inclusive to all spiritual paths without the destructive elements of self-serving, or power-hungry, "false spiritualists", in order to set forth a clear set of moral directives for all non-Christian, pagan, Wiccan, and neo-pagan religions. In April of 1974, the Council drafted the following principles which came to be called *The Thirteen Principles*:

Thirteen Principles

1. We practice rites to attune ourselves with the natural rhythm of life forces marked by the phases of the Moon and the seasonal Quarters and Cross Quarters.

2. We recognize that our intelligence gives us a unique responsibility towards our environment. We seek to live in harmony with nature, in ecological balance offering fulfillment to life and consciousness within an evolutionary concept.

3. We acknowledge a depth of power far greater than that is apparent to the average person. Because it is far greater than ordinary it is sometimes called "supernatural", but we see it as lying within that which is naturally potential to all.

4. We conceive of the Creative Power in the universe as manifesting through polarity - as masculine and feminine - and that this same Creative Power lies in all people, and functions through the interaction of the masculine and feminine. We value neither above the other, knowing each to be supportive of the other. We value sex as pleasure, as the symbol and embodiment of life, and as one of the sources of energies used in magical practice and religious worship.

5. We recognize both outer and inner, or psychological, worlds - sometimes known as the Spiritual World, the Collective Unconscious, Inner Planes, etc. - and we see in the interaction of these two dimensions the basis for paranormal phenomena and magical exercises. We neglect neither dimension for the other, seeing both as necessary for our fulfillment.

6. We do not recognize any authoritarian hierarchy, but do honor those who teach, respect those who share their greater knowledge and wisdom, and acknowledge those who have courageously given of themselves in leadership.

7. We see religion, magic and wisdom-in-living as being united in the way one views the world and lives within it - a world view and philosophy of life which we identify as Witchcraft, the Wiccan Way.

8. Calling oneself "Witch" does not make one a Witch - but neither does heredity itself, nor the collecting of titles, degrees and initiations. A Witch seeks to control the forces within her/himself that make life possible in order to live wisely and well without harm to others and in harmony with nature.

9. We believe in the affirmation and fulfillment of life in a continuation of evolution and development of consciousness, that gives meaning to the Universe we know, and our personal role within it.

10. Our only animosity towards Christianity, or toward any other religion or philosophy of life, is to the extent that its institutions have claimed to be "the only way," and have sought to deny freedom to others and to suppress other ways of religious practice and belief.

11. As American Witches, we are not threatened by debates on the history of the Craft, the origins of various terms, or the origins of various aspects of different traditions. We are concerned with our present and our future.

12. We do not accept the concept of absolute evil, nor do we worship any entity known as "Satan" or "the Devil", as defined by Christian tradition. We do not seek power through the suffering of others, nor do we accept that personal benefit can be derived only by denial to another.

13. We believe that we should seek within nature that which is contributory to our health and well-being.

Even though the Council disbanded later that year, these Thirteen Principles are widely accepted today by Pagans and Wiccans, both in North America and other parts of the world. In 1978, the 13 principles were added to the United States Army's Religious Requirements and Practices of Certain Selected Groups: A Handbook for Chaplains in a section on the Wiccan religion, under the direction of Rev. Dr. J. Gordon Melton. Later attempts to reconvene the Council failed in 2011 and 2015.

Chapter 4: Wiccan Rituals

Wicca is a religion based in nature, as such, there is a tendency for Wiccans to uphold a reverence for the Cycles of the Earth, planting and harvesting, and the phases of the moon. The changing seasons of the solar year were of the most importance to our ancestors, and so the days that most delineated those seasons were sacred to them.

The Wheel of The Year

The Wheel of The Year is a pictographic representation of the different Sabbats of the solar year. Due to this representation of the seasons, many Wiccans who are in the midst of celebrating a Sabbat say they are "Turning the Wheel". Various Wiccan practices and rituals are dependent on the type of Wicca that is right for the individual, as well as other factors, such as geography. While many of those who call themselves, Witches observe all eight festivals on The Wheel of The Year, others only celebrate four. While the freedom to observe and uphold the celebrations most sacred to ones-self is a key part of Wicca, it helps to know about all of them in order to make the best-informed decisions. Many Wiccans view the Sabbats as a time of celebration, and a chance to engage with their Wiccan communities in seasonal festivities. Eclectic Wiccans, and solitary practitioners also use these occasions as a chance to connect with other like- minded people of similar faiths and traditions, because of the sense of community they incite, without having to join a Circle or coven.

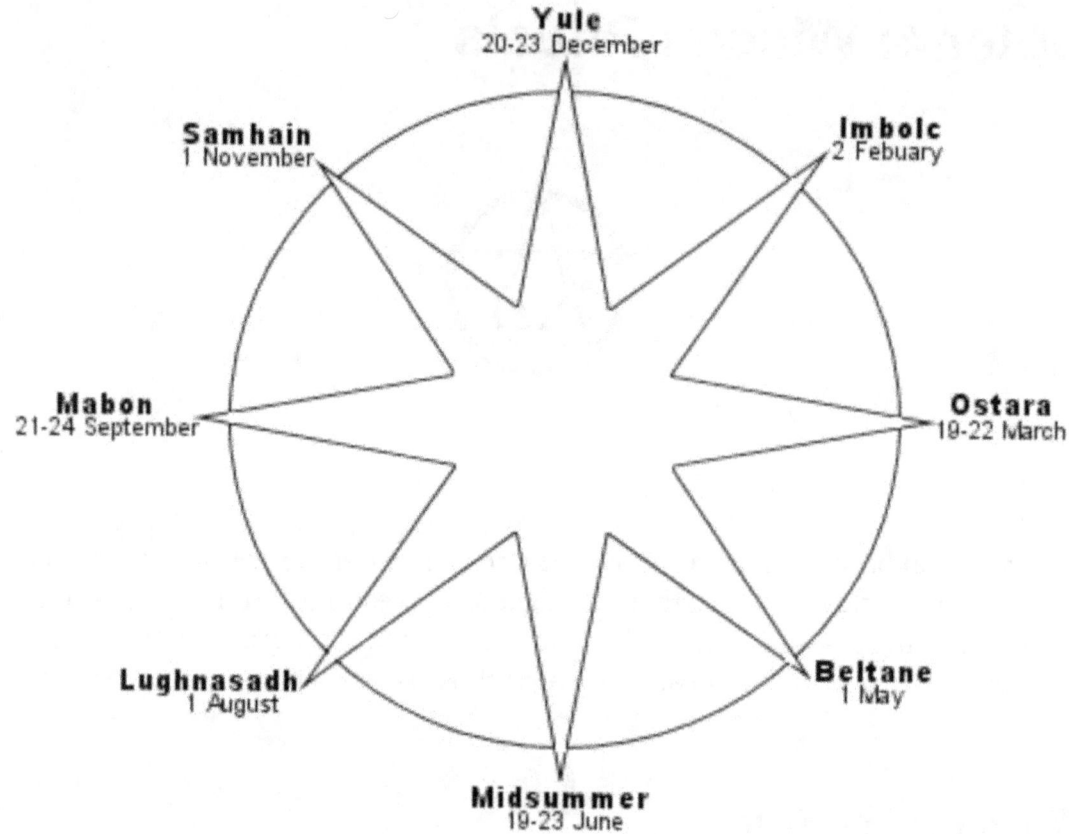

Sabbats

The Four main Solar events of the year are called either Solstices or Equinoxes. These events are also known as Quarter-days. A Solstice is when the sun reaches its highest point in the sky at noon, these are the longest days of the year. An Equinox is when the sun seems lowest in the sky at noon and are the seemingly shortest days of the Solar Year. There are two Solstices and two Equinoxes every year. In between these Sabbats are the Cross-quarter days. Sabbats also mark important times in the planting and harvesting cycles of the earth. Sabbats are festivals that celebrate the agricultural cycle and its notable times. These festivals are also times when the Wiccan practitioner honors the Male side of the Divinities for His protection, and virility in fertilizing the crops.

Solstices

The Winter Solstice, also called Yule generally happens between December 20-23. Yule is celebrated as both the beginning and the end of the solar year, depending on viewpoint and personal preferences. Wiccans honor the Winter Solstice because being the shortest day of the year with the longest night, it signifies a returning to the lighter half of the year, the darkest days are finally over, and the days will start to lengthen again. Yule is a time of hope, rebirth and regeneration. Yule is often marked with festivities like gift-giving and feasting, and homes, as well as altars, are often decorated with wintergreen boughs like holly, mistletoe, pine and yew. Early Christianization of Europe led to the Sabbat of Yule being absorbed, along with of its many customs, into Christianity. One can still see many of these traditions that have carried over from the old lore today.

Litha or the Summer Solstice happens between June 19-23. Litha is the solar opposite of Yule, being the longest day, and shortest night of the year, and it is often also called Midsummer. The Summer Solstice is honored as a time of plenty, with the crops growing well in the fields, the flora and fauna of the Forest and Wild places reaching the heights of productiveness and growth. Litha is a time of merriment for Wiccans, who gather to celebrate what is left of the bright Summer sunlight, knowing that Autumn is on its way.

Equinoxes

Equinoxes fall midway between the solstices on the Wheel of The Year. These Sabbats celebrate a time when things seem to be most "in balance" because the day and night are equal in length. The first of these occurs between March 19-22 and is the Vernal Equinox, also known as Ostara, or Eostar. This Sabbat is a time of hope and celebration for Wiccans when the grip of Winter loosens further. Ostara is a time of renewal and balance, and this Equinox is honored by looking at the world with the wonder of youth, as the earth and all of its creatures awaken from their slumbers of Winter.

Mabon is the Autumnal Equinox and takes place between September 21-24. This is a time for asking the blessings of the Divinities, and of sharing the bounties of the Earth. Because this Sabbat coincides with the final harvest of the season, Wiccans use it to celebrate and show thankfulness for the harvests and fruits of the earth, knowing that the long nights and barren days of Winter are coming. Alter decorations for the Fall Equinox includes acorns and the first turned leaves of the season, along with draping's or cloth in autumn colors like deep reds, oranges, dark yellow, and browns. This Sabbat underscores the need for balance in our work and recreational lives and was a much-needed day of rest for our agricultural ancestors.

Cross-Quarter Days

Along with the Solstices and Equinoxes, the Cross-Quarter Days on the Wheel of The Year generally mark significant days in the agricultural season. These four Sabbats are called Imbolc, Beltane, Lughnasadh, and Samhain, and are timed between the Solstices and Equinoxes.

The first of these, Imbolc, occurs between the Winter Solstice and the Vernal Equinox on February First or Second. Imbolc is a traditional time of cleansing and clearing out of the old, leftover things from Winter. Wiccans will organize their own lives, cleansing themselves physically, spiritually and in their personal lives, to make ready for the new year to come. Imbolc is a time of preparation, new beginnings, and imagination, creativity. Large feasts typically marked this Sabbat, along with an annual spring cleaning of one's home. Celebrations often involved divination, candles or bonfires. This Sabbat may even be a precursor to our own Groundhog Day, seeing as celebrants of Imbolc often participated in weather divination activities, such as watching to see if animals like snakes and badgers left their winter dens.

Beltane falls halfway between the Spring Equinox and Summer Solstice. Also known as May Eve, or May Day, and occurring on April 30 or May 1, Beltane is a joyous celebration, full of effervescent, lighthearted festivities. These festivities often include ritual bonfires, lit on the top of holy, or sacred hills to ward away negative energy, and ensure a bountiful planting season. Sometimes, twin bonfires would be lit, and people would either leap over the embers, pass between the fires, as well as drive cattle drive between them. As this solstice starts the planting season, Beltane also symbolizes Marriage, Unions, and Fertility. This means unions occurring during this festival are often considered to be auspicious, and certain to be fruitful! This Sabbat was also the time of year when livestock was traditionally driven out to their summer pastures, and many rituals for the Holy Day include wards and protections because of this to ensure a rewarding summer.

Lughnasadh, otherwise known as Lammas, is normally celebrated on August 1, although many Wiccans will vary this date slightly depending on familial or cultural tradition, and convenience. Lammas represented the very the first harvest, or the year's "First Fruits" (very often grains) and was considered both a time of joy for the coming harvest, as well as trepidation toward the coming of the long cold days of Winter. This is a time of preparation for Wiccans as they take stock of their lives on all levels and learn what areas need improvement to progress through the hardships of winter and protect themselves from negativity. Lammas is also known as Gathering Day in some traditions, as this is the time best suited for gathering herbs for healing and ritual. Some customs also include the ritual of the lighting of large wheels which were then rolled downhill into lakes or streams. This may be representative of the sun's cycle of rising and falling to remind us that although the Winter days are coming, the Wheel of the Year still turns, and the days of Summer won't be far behind.

The final Cross-quarter day is Samhain or All Hallows Eve. Samhain's ceremonies are held on October 31 or November 1, and many of its customs have carried over into today's Halloween festivities. Riding on the opposite side of the Wheel of The Year as Beltane, Samhain is considered to be a time to celebrate the accomplishments of the season and to pay respects to our Ancestors, those that have gone before us. Feasting, drinking, and contests of strength, ability and horse racing also marked this festival. Divination played a large part in Samhain celebrations, as well, from omens found in the smoke of ritual bonfires, to egg whites dropped in water and readings like tea leaves, many of these divinations were for matrimonial purposes. With the hope to see who the diviner might marry, or to find out if wealth and prosperity was in the future (or perhaps both!).

Esbats

Esbats are rituals and ceremonies that celebrate the Moon's cycle around the Earth. An Esbat is normally held for spell casting or spiritual reflection. This may serve as a very powerful time to hold a healing ceremony because of the healing nature of the Goddess. Esbats usually invoke and honor the Mother-Goddess.

The most commonly held Esbat is on the night of a Full Moon, and is considered a time for Covens to gather, and individual Wiccan practitioners to add their energies to the collective of positivity all around the world. The Lunar counterparts to the eight Sabbats, the Esbats are celebrated according to the thirteen lunar cycles that happen throughout a solar year, and these celebrations are often considered a "second", or as a reflection of, the Wheel of the Year. An opportunity for Wiccans to commune with the Triple Goddess in all her Divine forms, a Full Moon Esbat is the time to perform a Drawing Down the Moon ritual for many practitioners of The Craft.

These celebrations often vary widely in both their ritualistic components, as well as their timing, depending on purpose, cultural and geographic traditions. Wiccans consider the Lunar Holy Nights to be times of personal introspection and often solitary ritual. For these Wiccans, the Esbats are an opportune time for meditation and bathing in the loving light of the Mother's moon. Following the waxing and waning of the moon, the Esbats are said to be reflections of the Goddess' aspects of Maiden during the waxing phase of the moon, the Mother at the full moon and Crone for the waning phase. This cycle was considered to be sacred to the Goddess and time of power for all feminine energies because it followed nearly the same timing as a female's menstrual cycle, between twenty-eight and thirty days. When two full moons fall within the same month, it is called a Blue Moon Esbat, and workings done at these times are considered to be especially powerful since this Esbat heightens and amplifies all energies.

Chapter 5: The Wiccan Ritual & Magic

Although some Wiccan rituals are performed solely for the celebration of Sabbats and Esbats, many rituals include spells or energy workings for a variety of purposes, from spell casting and divination to hand-fasting, and funerals. These spells can be for healing, protection, banishing negative influences, fertility and initiation. Energy work is performed during a ritual to bring about change in the physical world through the manipulation and direction of the will.

Although the exact components may vary widely depending on the purpose, most Wiccan rituals follow (at least loosely) the same general pattern:

- Purification/Cleansing- The area that the ceremony will take place in, as well as the participants are cleansed of negativity and undesirable energies.

- Setting of the Altar- Even if a permanent altar is kept, it will often be decorated for the specific purpose/occasion, with the magical tools used for the ceremony laid upon it along with any offerings or other symbols.

- Casting of the Circle- The the circle creates a boundary between the participants of the ritual and the the outside world, keeping negativity and unwanted influences and energies out.

- Invocations- The Elements are called upon, often termed "Calling the Quarters", and the Divinities invoked to bless, participate in, and grant success to the ritual.

- Statement of Intent- This helps to focus both ritual and participant, keeping the energies and workings targeted on the objectives of the ceremony.

- Main Body- The main body of a ritual may be constituted of a variety of activities. These could be anything from re-enactment, poetry reading or singing, to spell casting, prayer, or naming a newborn. The activities during a ritual are as many reasons for holding one!

- Grounding and Centering- Often done with a practice called "Cakes and Ale" or "Cakes and Wine", this component of a ceremony gives thanks to the Gods, and prepares the participants for the closing of the circle and the end of the ritual.

- Finally, the Sacred Circle and Elements are released, the Divinities thanked, and the ritual is ended

Cleansing is the act of clearing away unwanted energies from a person, place or item. This means that anything can be Cleansed/ Purified, from the Athame you just bought from the store, your second-hand cauldron, buildings, rooms, ritual circles, even people! Ritual cleansing is the simple act of removing energy that can be perceived as negative or a negative influence, thereby keeping your environment and yourself in balance, focused and healthy. There are numerous ways to perform a cleansing or purification, some work better than others depending on what is being cleansed, and it benefits a Wiccan practitioner to learn a few (or many!) different methods.

Cleansing should be done before a ritual so that there are no negative, or unwanted energies within the ritual space. Make sure all of your ritual tools are consecrated, as well as the space your circle will be marked out. There are more ways to cleanse objects later on in the book, but some of the easiest are crystals and smudging. Many Wiccans will use their crystals for cleansing their ritual tools, a besom for the area of the ritual and sacred circle, and blessed water to consecrate the participants. It's a good idea to cleanse and/or purify the participants of your ritual, as well. If you plan on having more than one participant for your ritual, you can use any number of means to cleanse people, such as crystals, smudging, sound, or purified water. If you are performing a ritual in the privacy of your own home, a wonderful way to take advantage of your privacy, is to take a nice, relaxing bath before you start your ritual, some candles, or purifying crystals placed in your bathroom will do a great job of adding to the purifying energy and help get you into a relaxed mental state for your ritual, too. You can say a little prayer to the Goddess if you like, as you visualize Her blessings cleansing your mind, body and spirit of all the negativity within you. When you're done, thank Her, and simply rinse the unwanted energies down the drain. Some covens or groups will even bath together as a mass purification, but the means should be what feels right for you.

Intent and focus are the two key elements in creating a ritual or ceremony of your own. There is no "wrong" way to go about holding a ritual as long as you are sincere in your intent and focused on your goals and purpose for the ritual. Some techniques for meditation are given later on in chapter six because it is a fantastic way to hone your skills in focusing on your intent. Meditation can also help you with the intention of your ritual if you are unsure of it.

An altar is a structure that Wiccans use as a focal point in rituals, spell work, meditation and prayer. Many Wiccans use an altar made of wood, however, the type of wood used may differ between practitioners, depending on the purpose of the ritual, the environment, and of course, the individual Wiccan. The altar is often a very personal space that practitioners of magic like to keep their magic tools, and many keep their chalices, candles, athames, and pentacles upon their altars, to name just a few. There are many ways in which to place the items on your altar but remember to leave space for working a ritual or spell. Some witches even keep multiple altars for different purposes, such as a seasonal altar, decorated with seasonal flowers or holly and pine boughs as the Wheel turns, an altar for their ancestors, with pictures, and offerings to their grandparents and their grandparents, as well as a main altar where they keep tools, and perform their rituals. Your altar should be adorned depending on the casting or ritual or seasonally as you prefer. The seasonal decoration is normally done according to the Sabbats, the changing seasons, and the sowing and harvest cycles.

Wiccan rituals normally take place in what is called a magic circle. A magic circle is a boundary between the ritual being worked, and the outside, or mundane world. The circle is used to contain and concentrate the energies used in the ritual being worked. In order to cast your Circle, first, decide where you will cast it. A Sacred Circle is normally nine feet in diameter but can be as large or small as the caster chooses, as long as there is room enough inside for the participants to move freely while performing their ritual. Next, the area for the circle to be cast is cleansed and purified, to remove any energies that may interfere with the ritual. Once this has been done, you can then mark out your circle. If you are outdoors, natural elements may be used such as stones, many Circles are also marked out with chalk, salt, or cord laid out in the shape of your Circle and the ends tied. Next place all of your ritual components inside your Circle, it is traditional that your Altar is placed facing North, however many witches prefer theirs facing East, or in the direction of the Element, they feel most associated with. It is disruptive to the energies being worked in a ritual if the ritual has to be stopped, for whatever reason, so this is an important step and can prevent a frustrating delay if you have to stop and search for a tool or component. Trace your Circle energetically, either with your hand, athame, wand or besom as you walk deosil (clockwise) around the inside perimeter, some Wiccans recommend three times. When your ritual is finished, release your circle by walking widdershins, or counterclockwise, around it and visualize drawing your circle back into what you traced it out with, your hand, wand, or athame, for instance.

An evocation to the elements is the next step, although some Wiccans replace this with a ceremony called Calling the Quarters, and there are yet others who do both. As with much of Wicca, it's best to find the method that works for you. Evoking the Elements involves raising energy from the elemental forces of nature to make those energies available to the participants of a ritual. Invocation of the Gods is an important part of many ceremonies but should not be confused with evoking the Deities. Invocation is the act of calling upon the Gods or Elements and allowing them to manifest their presence through the person doing the invocation. Wiccans often use an Invocation of the Gods as a means of channeling Divine messages or intervention.

Evocation, on the other hand, is a more passive form of communing with the Gods and other spiritual entities. Evoking is achieved by calling upon the Divinities, or other forms of higher existence and asking for their presence without becoming a medium in the process. Wiccans use evocation in order to add to the spiritual energies during a working, create balance, stability and harmony of the energies used in the ceremony, and for the blessing and success of the ritual in process. It is common to evoke the Divinities and invoke the Elements, unless you are specifically communing with the deities in your ritual. This way the elements can work directly through you, and the Gods may lend their aid without having to manifest themselves through a participant of the ritual. After you have your Circle cast, mark out the Cardinal directions, and place a candle of the appropriate color for each or a physical representation such as a feather for Air, a bowl of soil or salt for Earth, a vessel of water for the Element of Water, and incense or a candle for Fire. Starting either in the North or East or in the direction your altar faces you should now invoke the Elements. To do this you can recite a chant of Invocation, play a specific musical instrument for each Element (flute for Air, string instruments for Fire, for Water use anything resonant like cymbals or a singing bowl, and drums for Earth) or simply ask for the Elements' aid in your ritual with a small prayer of welcome and request for their assistance as you walk clockwise again around the inside, stopping at each representation of an Element to invoke it. When the ritual is finished, one should Release the Quarters or Elements in the reverse direction that they were called.

After the Calling of the Quarters, a Statement of Intent is often made to focus the energies of the participants. This can be as simple or elaborate as you wish, depending on the occasion for the ritual. A simple statement at the beginning of the ritual is all that is truly needed. As discussed previously, there are a great many different types of Wiccan rituals, the one thing they all have in common, is intent. A ritual's intent is the reason that the ceremony is taking place. Rituals may have one intent or many. For instance, a celebration of the Vernal Equinox that contains a Naming Ceremony would be a ritual with dual intent or purpose. Keeping the intent of a ritual in mind will help to keep the ceremony progressing, as well as letting the participants of the rite know what energies they should be focused on. Many people write down the intent of a ritual and read it just after the Circle is cast. This lets the ritual begin even before the invocations and lets the participants of the ritual know what to focus their energy on, so they can immediately start building energy to perform the task. Even if you are performing your ritual alone, a Statement of Intent can keep you focused on the reason for the ritual. For instance, if your Statement of Intent goes something like "We are gathering tonight to celebrate the Full Moon, Draw Down the Goddess, and give our thanks to the Mother of All." Then everyone knows immediately that this will be a ritual of invocation and a celebration of honoring the Mother and can focus their energies on those Elements that pertain to Her.

When a witch uses the word "intent" referring to a ritual or spell, they are speaking about the goal, the reason the ritual or spell exists. Think of it this way, if you cast a healing spell, your intentions are to heal the target of your spell work, but that isn't necessarily what the Intent of the spell is. The *intent* of the spell could be much more specific, such as clearing away a cold or infection in the lungs, alleviating pain, or settling a stomach. The more you fine-tune your *Intent*, the more likely it will be that you'll be able to focus more energy into the spell or ritual. It isn't always that important to focus that closely, for instance, if you are gathered at a group celebration for the Summer Solstice, the intent of the central ritual may simply be to give thanks to the Gods and be merry. The intent behind the Sabbat ritual, in this case, doesn't need to be so finely fixed, because it isn't so difficult to be merry or give thanks. As long as you are earnest in your gratitude to the Divinities, and enjoy the communion of your fellow Wiccans, you have accomplished the goals of the ritual. In the healing spell example, however, you will want to choose the finest point on your intentions as you possibly can. This creates an area to direct our energies so that we won't waste them directing them to somewhere not needed. Of course, if you inadvertently send soothing energies to the lungs, as you try and settle the stomach, it won't hurt the subject, but your spell may not be as effective because you have essentially "watered down" the concentration of your healing energies.

Once the invocations, evocations and Statement of Intent are done, it is finally time to perform the main body of the ritual. This is the part of a ceremony where spells are cast, hand-fastings are sealed, and the Sabbats are celebrated. The main body of the ritual is the focal point of the ceremony and may consist of a variety of activities. In the Drawing Down the Moon example above, the High Priestess, or solitary Wiccan would stand in the Goddess pose, which is arms upward, and feet close together, in a "Y" formation. and recite the Drawing Down of the Moon poem. The Charge of the Goddess often follows, with the Priestess in a trance-like state and channeling The Goddess. Another example would be Raising a Cone of Power. This is a ritual enacted by a group of Wiccan practitioners and involves the participants calling up energy as they gather around the magic circle and concentrating that energy on a focal point centered above the group, thus forming a cone. When the cone has been raised to full power, the participating members then visualize sending that cone towards their goal and adding immense amounts of the energy toward the accomplishment of it. Notable examples of a Cone of Power being raised would be the New Haven's efforts in Raising a Cone in 1940 in order to prevent Germany from invading Great Britain, or California gathering that raised a Cone of Power with the intent to stop the Vietnam War.

When the main body of the ritual has been done, it is time to release the energies you have evoked. This is normally done with a prayer and a word of thanks to the Gods you have called upon for aid and blessings. Release the Quarters, and your magic circle, this creates a sense of closure for the participants, and lets them relax their mental focus, and finally you're ready to ground and center yourself to get rid of any unwanted energies.

The act of grounding is similar to a meditational exercise, in that the unwanted, pent up energy within is visualized as leaving the body or being pushed out. Often, someone in the act of grounding will imagine themselves as having roots that go deep into the earth, when they ground their energies, they visualize all the excess energy and negativity as being pushed down through the "roots" and into the earth where it can then return to a neutral state. Grounding and centering are both useful tools for manipulating our energy, Centering for drawing in, and Grounding for expelling. Centering will also help you with focusing on your intent. All too often, our daily lives make us feel "stretched too thin", overwhelmed, or forgetful. When we feel this way, it's usually because we are not centered correctly within ourselves. Centering is the act of pulling back your energy, from whatever may be draining on them, it is literally the act of coming back to center, that space where you are at peace, calm and collected whether it's work stress, bills piling up, or just a general feeling of disconnectedness, and bringing those energies back to within yourself, or your "center". It's much more difficult to be distracted from your ritual's intent if you have properly centered yourself.

Wiccan Magic

There is a vast range of magical traditions that have been passed down from our ancestors, many of which are still being practiced in some form. Wiccan magic calls upon many of its origins from European and ancient Hermetic practices, some of which helped to introduce Western Europeans to Astrology and Alchemy. Wiccans believe that the energies that enable a person to shape and manifest their destiny according to their will are present in everyone. This means that Magic, in and of itself, isn't supernatural at all, it is just a misunderstanding of natural law. The ability to use magic and manipulate the energies of the natural world are simply a heightened level of consciousness. One that we can all gain.

At its very core Wiccan magic is a very personal, experimental art, that should be explored by the solitary practitioner fully, in order to discover the path that works best for the manifestation of their will. Magic is believed by many Wiccans to be a natural phenomenon, much like gravity, or wind; it exists, all around us as a part of nature, but is unable to be seen by the untrained naked eye. It is a part of the natural world, and thus, not supernatural at all. Wiccans use Magic and Witchcraft as tools to influence the environment and elements around them, often with the aid of rituals, ceremonies, meditation, and/or spells. This allows a witch to harness and manipulate the elements and forces around themselves, much like a windmill is used to harness the power of the wind to cause a beneficial result.

Witchcraft is most easily defined as a manipulation of the energetic forces existing both within and outside of one's self by exercising and focusing one's will, most often through the use of meditation, ritual, and/or spells. The majority of Witchcraft is based in and around the forces and elements of nature. Many of its components are used to represent, recreate, or draw one closer to an understanding of the natural world around us. This gives Wiccans have a deep respect for the elements, environment, and a balanced view of their place in Creation.

There is such an incredibly diverse array of magical practices, one could not hope to touch on everyone in a single lifetime. There is also an abundant number of magical components and materials used in Wiccan rituals. As noted previously, experimentation is needed to discover what works best for you. It is important to realize, that as a novice practitioner, or even as an Adept, the only real schedule in Wiccan magic is the Wheel of The Year! There aren't any real checkpoints that a practitioner must pass to become a Wiccan, other than simply declaring one's self, or being initiated into Wicca. Taking your time, researching, and experimenting are the most important, for these will lead you to the path that suits you best!

Some of the most commonly used, simple, and easily practiced Magical Arts are also wonderful learning tools for the beginning Wiccan practitioner.

Candle Magic

Candle magic makes for excellent visualization and manifestation exercise in that it helps to teach the concepts of Intent and transformation of energies by connecting with the Fire Element. Candle magic also offers a non-intimidating and straightforward introduction to performing rituals in general, since all that is essentially required are the altar, circle and candles needed to perform a spell. This Craft uses colored candles and paper to align energies according to one's will. Colors of candles correspond with different purposes in candle magic. Although some colors and intentions will vary between casters and traditions, and there are more correspondences than space permits, some of the more popular are:

- White- purity and eliminating negativity
- Black- protection and repelling negative energies
- Red- love, vitality and courage
- Purple- spirituality and wisdom
- Blue- meditation, healing and happiness
- Green- Financial matters, wealth and success
- Yellow- manifestation of the will and creativity
- Orange- joy and positive energy

When performing a simple candle magic spell, use the colored candle that corresponds with the type of spell you will be casting, purify and anoint it either with olive oil you have purified, or an appropriate scented essential oil. Some candle magics also call for your candle to be rolled in dried and powdered herbs as well. You will also want a piece of paper that is of the same color as your candle. Cast your circle around your altar, you can call the Quarters, but with such a small spell, and the candle doing most of the work, it is not always necessary. Once this is done, set your intention, and write it down on the paper. For example, if you are casting a healing spell, use a blue candle, and a blue piece of paper. You would then write your intention along the lines of "Sally will be free of her hay fever" on the piece of paper. As you write down your intention, visualize the outcome (Sally, on a green lawn, happy and not sneezing). See in your mind's eye all the different ways that your will may manifest, such as Sally finally getting that prescription she's been needing, or her husband finally cutting down that ragweed tree outside their doorway. Close your eyes and keep the focus on your intent as you fold the paper. Some Wiccans like to voice an incantation or prayer at this point, and you can even make one up for your spell, such as "My friend Sally shall be well, this, the reason for my spell, Let her be allergy-free, as I will it, so let it be!" Allow one corner of the paper to catch fire in the candle's flame, and burn as much as possible, without burning yourself. When you can no longer hold the paper, place it in your cauldron, or another fire-safe spot to burn the rest of the way through. Allow the candle to fully burn down, usually, there will be a small stub left, and you may dispose of this by either burying it or simply discarding. Never use a candle twice, or reconstitute them, the fire element has already used that one, meaning its energies will be too far depleted to be of use in another spell.

Crystal Magic

Crystals, semi-precious stones, rocks and minerals have long been used in Wiccan energetic workings and rituals. Crystals and stones are thought to be vessels of energy, and as alive as any other part of nature, and are often used in healing workings, scrying and divination. Advantages of crystal magic are that gemstones are easy to come by, cleansed, and consecrated so materials for these spells are usually not expensive. Crystals, like candles, have different correspondences when performing spell work with them. Some of the more widely used are:

- Amethyst- used for focusing intent, healing, and energetic cleansing

- Bloodstone- healing, wealth and fertility

- Citrine- self-confidence and dream interpretation

- Hematite- increases logic and reason and absorption of negativity

- Jade/Aventurine- harmony, balance and wealth

- Moonstone- intuition, healing and connects with the Goddess

- Rose Quartz- love, friendship and also self-healing

Crystals are often purified and charged with a specific intent, then carried with a person for the effect desired, placed on an altar to absorb or add to energies pertaining to the ritual being performed. Some are even etched with Runes and read as a divinatory tool. Crystals are a useful, and versatile magical tool, that wise witches take full advantage of! You'll learn more later about purifying and cleansing with crystals, as well. A very simple way to take advantage of crystal magic is to use them in conjunction with other magics, such as candles. Let's use our example from above to help Sally with her hay fever with the added benefits of crystal energy. Before you begin your candle spell, have a cleansed piece of amethyst on hand, and place it in front of your candle before your ritual begins. Amethyst is a crystal that helps promote and boost energies. This means that it will act as an amplifier for your energy work, creating a more powerful effect. You'll also want a small piece of bloodstone, clear quartz or sodalite. After your statement of intent, when you light the paper, pass your small bloodstone, or whichever healing crystal you may have chosen, through the smoke created by the candle and burning paper. Visualize your intentions being absorbed by the stone and charging it with healing energy. Once the paper has burned, and your spell is completed, the bloodstone can then be given to Sally as a healing talisman. It will work sort of like a mobile energy boost, in that your intentions will be carried with her, no matter where she goes. This will, in turn, help the channels you created for your spell open wider to the manifestation of your will by simply being in close proximity.

Herbal Magic

Herbs are also used in many ways throughout Wiccan magic. From poppets and charms to incense and teas, Herbal magic is some of the most widely used and versatile magic being practiced by Wiccans. Herbal magic is also easy to start out with since most people have some of its components right in their kitchens! Whether you burn a smudge stick made of sage to ward away negativity or drink a chamomile tea to relax after a hard day, this Art is one of the easiest to incorporate into daily life. There are many herbs used in and as an aid to other forms of magic as well. Some of these uses include scented oils used on candles for candle magic, and incense used in many other spells of various natures, herbs can also be used in Cauldron magic for brewing potions. Herblore is perhaps one of the most widely used magical practices in Wicca. Some more common Herbal equivalents:

- Financial, and business- Sandalwood, basil, clover, pennyroyal
- Good luck- Hazel, pomegranate, sunflower
- Health and healing- Comfrey, chamomile, peppermint
- Love- Lavender, yarrow, apple blossom
- Protection- Aloe Vera, thistle, mandrake, mistletoe

An easy way to incorporate herbs into your spell casting can also be done with candle magic. Let's go back to Sally again in our candle spell. Comfrey is a healing herb, so have some dried, and crushed into a powder before you start. Now, right after you've anointed your candle, roll it gently in the powdered comfrey to coat it with the herb. Then proceed as you normally would with your spell. The healing qualities of the comfrey will permeate your candle magic, adding even more healing properties to your components, so you have once again added to the energetic qualities of the original spell you cast.

Divination

Divination is the Craft of seeing what the future holds. Whether through the Tarot, Norse Runes, I-Ching, or tea leaves, witches and mystics have been peering through the veil of time to gain answers to questions of what is in store for them, to more accurately guide or understand our Fate. The power to know what will happen to an individual is an alluring ability, but many who practice divination regularly, will tell you that no future is set in stone, and we can guide ourselves through anything we "see" during divining with intuition, and responsibility.

Tarot

Tarot cards are one of the most widely known and common divinatory tools and are easily found in several stores, as well as online. Just as with any magic tool, make sure you cleanse your divination medium (your tarot deck, I-Ching coins or rune set, for instance) before you use them so that there are no unwanted or negative energies residing in them. The Tarot is a deck of cards originally used in the fifteenth century as playing cards, which later on, in the eighteenth century, became popular for divination. Each Tarot deck uses a Major Arcana of twenty-one cards, to symbolize the Greater Secrets, cards such as Strength, The High Priestess, and Temperance cards, are used for broad meanings in a reading, such as the Tower symbolizing great and chaotic change. Fifty-six Minor Arcana cards are divided into four suits, usually Wands, Cups, Pentacles, and Swords. These suits correspond with the Four Earthly Elements, namely Fire, Water, Earth and Air, worldly attributes that are combined with the numbered cards in each suit (Ace through ten plus a King, Queen, Knight and Page) which represent smaller aspects of the base Elements. For instance, the suit of Wands usually represents the Fire element, and aces in each deck normally symbolize the generating aspects of each suit, so your ace of Wands would stand for the initiatory properties of Fire, such as creativity, passion, and drive. When performing a Tarot layout, consider the query you have. This is just like a *statement of intent*, only you can think of it instead as a question of intent. Once you have your question, hold your cards while either breathing on them, or say a small prayer confirming your intention, and asking for the Divinities' help. Tarot readings have many various layouts that give both in-depth or very simple readings, from three-card layouts, representing Past Present and Future, to eleven card spreads that give a detailed reading of many aspects of a querent's life. Generally, it's best to pick a layout that will answer your question most thoroughly. when you have made your intent known to your oracle, draw your cards and place them face-up on the reading surface. These cards are then interpreted according to the placement of them and the symbolic positions they hold in the areas of which the layout pertains. For instance, if you find the Hanged Man in the position of money and finances, you may interpret this card as meaning that money will come to the person in question, but it will be within time. Another variation is to lay all cards face down their positions, and read each one individually as you flip each card in turn. If you choose the second variation, make sure to flip the cards over without changing their up and down orientation, in other words, flip them over like you would the pages of a book, Tarot cards have different meanings when they land inverted.

Runes

Norse runes are an ancient alphabet originating in Scandinavia. Most commonly carved onto slips of wood, but often made of clay, ceramic, bone, or even etched into rock or semi-precious stones, twenty-four individual runes make up a set. Each rune has a symbol and phonetic value, that are used in divination to interpret concepts of the deeper, or lower, consciousness. The Isa (ee-sah) rune, for instance, has a shape that is simply a straight vertical line, symbolizing an icicle, or glacier, this would be ascribed to the Lower Conscious as immobility, and pressure, signifying great changes happening under the surface of conscious thought. Runes are used by a caster, or rune reader, in a similar fashion to tarot cards. The rune reader breaths the question into the runes, while asking for guidance from the divine. Each rune is then drawn out of the bag or box they are kept in, and individually placed in the reading positions. The rune reader then interprets these symbols, again, in a similar fashion to the Tarot. Another variation of rune reading is the casting method. After breathing the question to the runes, the reader will cast, throw, or drop the runes of the set onto a casting area, usually a cloth that has been embroidered, or marked with the symbolism of the caster's spiritual preferences. The runic symbols are then interpreted by the reader according to how they relate to the subject of the reading and how they lie in relation to each other. Just as in Tarot, the runes have different meanings depending on whether they land inverted or upright, so if you turn one over flip it like a book, from side to side, rather than end to end. For the casting method, you will only be reading the runes that were cast inside your circle marked upon the surface. Some rune readers also only read the runes that land face up as well. If, for instance the Isa symbol was cast in close proximity to the rune symbolizing the torch and wisdom (Kaw-nawz), then you would know that the changes happening in the subconscious mind relate to wisdom, and the learning of new, philosophical ideas that take time in order to "show up" on the surface of the consciousness.

Astrology

Many Wiccans practice Astrology as well. While Astrology is a type of divination, it encompasses much more, such as auspicious times of the year to perform certain workings. Two types practiced widely, those are Western and Chinese, or Eastern, Astrology. Western Astrology uses the movements of the celestial bodies such as the sun, moon and planets to divine events and relationship dynamics from the placement of these celestial bodies (sun, moon, planets) as they travel through twelve divisions of the sky, or "Houses", at the time of birth. The Western Astrology then uses these placements to discern the characteristics of the twelve Zodiac Signs, named for constellations, that correspond with each House. Western astrology goes further to then-Associate each astrological sign of the zodiac with one of the Elements, Air, Fire, Water or Earth, which then adds its characteristics to the individuals. a Fire sign, like Leo for instance, would generally have more of Fire's tendencies, such as large amounts of energetic passion and assertiveness, than a Water sign like Cancer, who might be more reserved, and emotional. Eastern Astrology uses 12 animal signs, rather than constellations, to give characteristics according to a year of birth, the lunar month, and two hours daily periods throughout each day. This creates a repetitive, cycle that repeats every twelve years. If someone was born in the year 2007, for instance, Eastern Astrology would place them in The Year of the Boar. This would also be the case for those born in the years 2019, and 2031, as well. The Eastern version of Astrology correlates the zodiac with Elements as well, but rather than the Western's four, the Eastern version uses the Elements of Metal, Wood, Fire, Earth and Water, and assigns them each to different years. This gives each Animal sign one of five different Element types, depending on that year's Elemental, which cycles every sixty years. Eastern Astrology readings are done to determine the fate and destiny of an individual and are still widely used for insight into marriage proposals and relationship advice.

Types of Witchcraft

You have seen a few of the different types of magic now, but there are also different types of witches as well. Just because someone is Wiccan, doesn't mean they are a witch, or even if they are, it doesn't necessarily mean that they would practice the same type of witchcraft as another witch.

Gardnerian witches follow the Gardnerian Tradition of Wicca and are formally initiated into their Craft by another Gardnerian. These witches have degrees of initiation they must pass to progress in their witchcraft. They also follow very structured rituals and methods of witchcraft and use a Book of Shadows descended directly from Gerald Gardner's original coven.

Alexandrian Witches also follow a Tradition of witchcraft that is derived from British Traditional Wicca. Although not quite as structured as Gardnerian witches, and incorporating elements of Qabalah and ceremonial magic, an Alexandrian witch must still be initiated into her coven and follow steps of passage to progress in The Craft.

Sea witches practice an eclectic for of Wicca and derive much of their energy for spell work from the Element of Water. A sea witch will often live close to or somewhere they have easy access to the ocean. These witches often use seashells, bits of driftwood, sea salt and sand during rituals as well as in spell casting and can sometimes have a knack for weather magic. Most sea witches you find will have a strong affinity with the Water Element.

A kitchen witch is one you will often find in the home. This type of witch leans heavily on herbal lore and uses a multitude of herbs in their practice of The Craft. Also known as a hearth witch, a Wiccan practicing this branch of witchcraft relies on her intuition to combine herbs, food, essential oils, and everyday items found around the home to incorporate in their Craft. Hearth witches are normally Masters of brewing potions, healing magic and nurturing their communities.

An elemental witch practices their tradition according to the four elements of nature, and uses the energies provided by them to work their Craft. Elemental witches often have a separate altar for each Element and uses the one most closely affiliated with the ritual or spell work to be done.

Hedge Witches practice an Eclectic Tradition of Wicca, and specialize in Astral travel, spirit journeying and herb lore in much the same way a shaman does. Taken from historical terminology, a "hedge" defined the borders between lands. A hedge witch, also known sometimes as a hedge rider, therefore, is someone who sees "both sides of the borders" of the Spirit world and our own, a Wiccan that practices hedge-witchery is said to be able to "lift the veil" between this world and the Spirit realm. A Wiccan who Rides the hedge will often practice dream interpretation, as well as a form of shamanic shapeshifting. These solitaries use meditation, trance states, and astral projection to communicate with energies, spirits, and the forces of nature to work their Tradition of The Craft. Hedge witches often practice herbal medicine, and most will keep their gardens or "hedges". Hedge riders also tend to know most of the local plant and animal lore specific to their geographical locations, and can often be found in the roles of healer, seer, and advisor to the surrounding community These witches sometimes have an affinity for weather magic as well, such as calling up rain. Many hedge witches are what the old stereotypical "wise woman living out in the woods" are based on because these Wiccans tend to be more solitary in their practices, as well as helpful in their healing abilities, and sharing in nature and lore. Most often not belonging to a specific coven, hedge witches can still be found among temporary Circle gatherings, often to celebrate a Sabbat, and take part in the sense of community, these gatherings offer to solitary practitioners.

Green witches practice a version of witchcraft similar to a hedge witch but concentrate on the elements and lore of nature rather than the more shamanistic hedge witch. A green witch will not necessarily use astral projection or spirit journeys and does not claim to "lift the veil" to the Otherworld. Instead, the green witch will use all the elements and lore of nature to protect and nurture the Earth. Many green witches are also environmental activists in their communities and work towards a healthy balance with Nature.

Hereditary witches are those who practice their Craft as it was handed down to them by their ancestors. A hereditary witch inherits the Craft when it is passed down through their family, creating a Tradition that is unique and can be passed down to their children. A hereditary witch must be born into their Tradition but does not have to practice witchcraft if not inclined to.

Cosmic Witches use the Stars, moon and planets to time, order and practice witchcraft. Sometimes called star witches, they are well versed in Astrology, Astronomy, and the secrets of the night sky. If one needs to know which constellation is in the House of Leo this month, or when the next new moon will be, it's usually a good bet that your local star witch will know the answers.

Secular witches practice magic separately from their spirituality. A secular witch is someone who practices magic but attaches no deities or spiritual significance to their work. Seculars can be religious but separate their Faith (if they practice one) from any magic they do. To a secular witch, the Craft is simply a means to direct their will, and they don't acknowledge that there are energies behind the Elements involved.

Tech Witch, a new term for many Wiccans, and can be described as a term for a witch that incorporates modern-day electronic, or other technologies not otherwise included, into their Traditions and practices. Many of these Wiccans believe that our ancestors made do with dangerous flames on candles or watching the sky for three days to find out whether the moon is waxing or waning, because they HAD to, not because they would have wanted to, given other options. These witches are more concerned with the value of technology when placed in a Wiccan or ritualistic situation than they are with outdated, and preconceived notions of Tradition. Some examples would be a Wiccan practitioner who transcribes their Book of Shadows onto a disc or hard drive or using a plug-in diffuser for essential oils. Other tech witches use mobile apps that tell them when the moon phases are or electric candles and Christmas lights for meditation. Tech witches are Wiccans who believe that technology isn't necessarily a negative thing to add to Wicca and that Nature can still be honored through the use of it. From using a black computer screen for a scrying mirror to the use of an electric kettle in place of a cauldron for brewing, tech witches are "the new breed" of Wiccans, and are helping Wicca to grow, and adapt for the Future.

The Five Elements

The Five Elements are Air, Fire, Water, Earth, and Aether, also known as Spirit. These Elements are used to describe and explain patterns, both in the natural world around us and within ourselves. The Five Elements are also manipulated for use in The Craft, and during rituals to add to our energies. The Elements are embodiments of the raw forces of nature and reside everywhere in the world around us. Knowledge of The Five Elements is an intrinsic part of understanding Wicca and Witchcraft, as well as being necessary to manipulate those Elements to successfully perform spells and work rituals. When we connect with the Elements, we are recognizing the reflections of those energies within ourselves, and the way those energies work with and respond to those around us. This may sound complicated, but it is very instinctual. When you are tired but need to get through two more hours of work before getting to go home, you may try and get yourself "fired-up". This is another way of saying you're inviting more Fire energy in so that you can harness that Elemental spirit to give you that boost you need. If you've ever commented that someone you know is "well-grounded" you've unconsciously recognized that that person seems to have an affinity for the Earth Element.

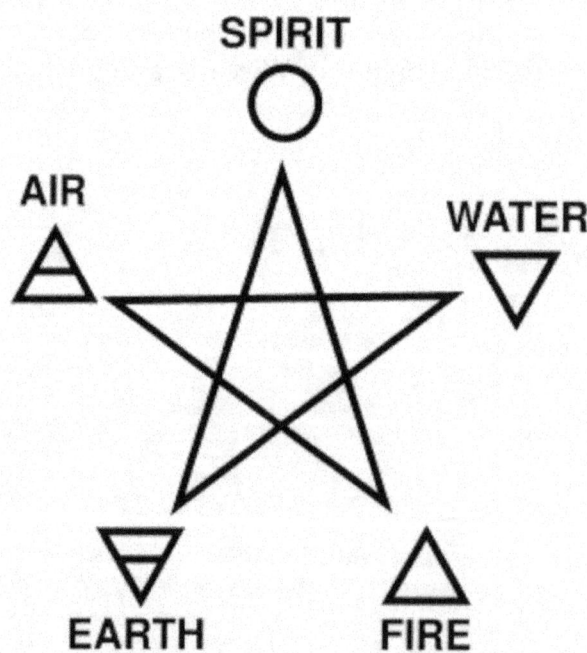

Each Element has a symbol, used in rituals and spell work to represent the Element, as well as in some forms of magical writing. Compass point (although this will vary between different Wiccans and geographical locations), as well as herbal, and tree correspondences. Each Element except for Aether has either a masculine or feminine correspondence as well. This means that the qualities of a specific Element will correlate with either passive (feminine) or active (masculine) tendencies. Fire, for instance, takes on masculine qualities in its tendency to destroy, but is still a force of creativity, when what has been destroyed was not beneficial. Earth, on the other hand, is feminine, and this Element's creative methods are passive evidenced by the steady cycle of growth, nurtured by the soil. It is a good idea to meditate on each Element individually, to gain a deeper understanding, and attain a harmonious balance of the Elements within one's self. The Five Elements are best illustrated as the five points of a pentagram, as in the example above, and are an important part of Wiccan rituals.

The element of Air exerts control over the powers of the mind. These areas include Knowledge, Communication, Ideas, Intelligence, and Inspiration. Air can be invoked during rituals by releasing an object into the wind, through fragrance or aromatherapy, or vocalizations such as singing or chanting. Air's gender is masculine, giving this element the creative power to incite new ideas, but also to sweep them away. An overabundance of the Air element within a person could lead to hard, cold rationality, with little room for emotion and compassion. His colors are yellow, white and crimson. This Element is placed on the Elemental Pentagram on the upper left point, and its corresponding compass direction is East, the Direction of new beginnings. When invoking this element specifically, the most auspicious times are Spring and dawn. Trees and herbs that have an affinity with Air are hazel, maple, pine, linden; and clove, myrrh, vervain, and parsley. Magic tools used to call upon Air are the censer (for burning incense), wand, and sword, this Elemental is most often used in divination, prophecy, visualization, and works involving Karmic Debt. The element of Air should be included in spell work involving teaching, knowledge, and travel. Air is also useful in visualization, and for boosting energies of the mind, like logical deduction and development of the psychic abilities. If you want to connect better with this Element, try meditating on your breathing, or sit quietly in a place where you can feel and hear the wind blow.

The next element is Fire, the driving force behind passion, love, energy, leadership, and inspiration. The Fire element can be invoked by burning objects, baking things, fires, and the lighting of candles. Fire's colors are red, gold, orange, crimson and white, and his gender is masculine, Fire is both creative and destructive. The compass point associated with Fire is South, and the best times for workings with a Fire nature are the Summer season and noon. Trees that embody the Fire Element are alder, ash, cedar, oak, holly and rowan. Some herbs with an affinity for Fire are garlic, red peppers, beans, cinnamon, coffee and seeds. Invocation tools for the elements of Fire are daggers or swords, athames, censers, candles, and burning herbs, such as smudge sticks. This Element is often called upon in candle magic, healing, energy-work, either to boost or balance the internal energies, and love spells by burning or heating of objects, and cauldron work. The sun and sunlight are also embodiments of this Element with their warming, healing qualities. Fire is a transformative Element, meaning that its energies change what it comes into contact with. Candle magic is a good example of this, as the Fire Element transforms the candle, paper, and intention of the spell being cast into energy to be directed. This Element is most active and is good to meditate on if you are feeling a lack of energy to perform a task. The Element of Fire is what brings light to dark places, this makes it a wonderful warding or banishing agent.

Water is the third Element and holds sway over emotion, purification, movement, wisdom and love. The Water element can be called upon by pouring water, the immersion of an object, brewing, and ritual bathing or cleansing. Water is feminine in nature and is mutable, changing shape according to the vessel which contains it. This Element has connections to the subconscious and can be used to connect with our deepest emotions. She is represented by the colors blue, turquoise, green, grey, indigo and black. This Element sits at the upper right point of the Elemental Pentagram and rules the Western compass point. Water rituals often take place in the Autumn and at twilight/dusk. The apple, birch, alder, elm and willow trees are representative of this Element. Herbs that correspond to her are ferns, water lotus, mosses, and gardenias. Some tools for summoning Water energy are cups, cauldrons, goblets and mirrors. Water is used in divination, healing, cleansing, and protection spells, frequently by the use of ritual bathing or cleansing, pouring and/or sprinkling water, or as a scrying medium. Springs, lakes, the ocean, wells, rivers, fog, rain and seashells are symbolic of the Water element. The Water Element is often used for lucid dreaming and trance magic and is often used to symbolize emotions hiding beneath the surface of our conscious. To connect more deeply to the Water Element, try walking in the rain, or spending time meditating next to a clear body of water.

The fourth element is Earth, which rules over strength, stability, prosperity, abundance, and money/financial matters. Invocation of the Earth Element is commonly done by burying objects, making likenesses, or effigies from wood or clay, and the act of planting. Earth is also a feminine Element, and shows her nurturing creative tendencies by being fertile, and producing new life. Black, brown, yellow, and green are Her colors. On the Elemental Pentagram, Earth sits at the lower left point and will be found in the North quadrant on a compass. Earth is generally called on using pentacles, pentagrams, salt, stones and gems, and is often invoked during the Wintertime and night, most successfully at midnight. Herbs that symbolize this element are ivy, grains, oats and rice, lichens and patchouli. Some trees that represent this element are cypress, walnut, hawthorn and oak. Earth is customarily used for grounding, money spells, rune casting, binding works, crystal magic, and Herbalism. The very rocks, soil, and fields embody Earth, as well as clay, caves, and natural salts. Earth is the closest Element to our physical bodies, and thus, is easy to connect with. To become more in tune with this Element, one can walk barefoot on the ground, or plant seedlings.

Spirit, or Aether, is the fifth element. Unlike the other four, this element is present in **all** living things, and is essential to the balance and connectivity of the other four elements, both around us and within ourselves. Spirit is invoked no matter what sort of ritual or spells are cast because it is the force that allows us to connect with the other elements. Aether is the bridge between our mind and the Divinities, as well as that between the elements and ourselves. It also connects Wiccan practitioners with both the Lower (or Sub-) Conscious, and the Higher Conscious (that which communicates with the Divine) which helps us to receive inspiration and insight. Aether is a gender-neutral element and is invoked by using any magical tool. This element sits at the very top of the Elemental Pentagram, showing its connectivity to all the other elements. Rather than being represented by a specific season, Spirit is symbolized by the Wheel of The Year in its entirety. The colors for this element are white, black, or black and white in combination, optionally a rainbow, representing all colors can be used. The Spirit Element can be represented by a spiral showing the endless movement around us of the Aether, or prism that changes white light into a spectrum. Aether is sometimes used specifically for opening the Third Eye, or "tuning in" to one's psychic senses, and in rituals that require a change like something. The Spirit Element is accessed by meditation on Divine guidance and the Divine within ourselves.

When the Elements are invoked during rituals, we are asking the energies themselves, the Elemental spirits, so to speak, to join in our rite, and participate in any magic work being done. This is because the Elements are an intrinsic part of everything we do, being the force of nature itself we can interact with, that bind all things into the cycles of life, death and rebirth. Most people find that they have a natural affinity for at least one of the Elements. If you were constantly playing in puddles, streams and pools as a child, you might have an affinity for Water. An Air inclination often shows up as someone who is uncannily logical for their age, etc. This makes for a good starting point for educating yourself about, identifying, and interacting with the Elements. While walking on a bright day, feel the warm sun on your face as you acknowledge it as the healing energy of the Fire element. When you dip your fingers into a stream or pool, feel the Water Element flowing around you. These exercises are ways you can start interacting with and building your connections to the Elements. You will come to discover that the more conscious you become of the Elements, the easier it is to bring them into balance within yourself. As you progress along your spiritual path, you will also become more adept at identifying the Elements and manipulating their energies.

Magical Tools

The Wiccan's altar is raised structure or place, used for ritual, casting spells, meditation and centering, and sits at the heart of a witch's sacred space. The altar is also the spot where they may place their ritual tools, offerings, and symbols. Because of this sacred nature, care and forethought should be used in setting up your altar. While there are some general guidelines for setting up your altar, there are no real absolute rules, and doing so should remain an intimate, personal and intuitive choice. All magical tools should be cleansed and consecrated before use in a ritual, to ensure that they are free of any negative energies. There is a multitude of tools used in Wiccan rituals, each designed to direct energies, often those of specific Elements, to perform a particular function. Some of the most commonly used tools in Wicca are:

- Pentacle, also known as a Paten- This is a disk or plate with a sigil on it, often engraved, and in Wicca, most often a Pentagram with a circle around it. Other symbols are used depending on the deities invoked and/or personal preference. This Disk represents the Element of Earth during rituals.

- Athame- A ritual sword or knife that has been consecrated and represents the Element of Air. The Athame is used to direct energy and control spirits, among other ritual purposes, but is not used for any actual physical cutting.

- Wand- The Wand represents the Element of Fire, and can be made from any material including wood, metal or rock, as long as it is a material found in Nature. The wand is often set with precious or semi-precious stones or engraved with sigils, or other symbols of power, and is often used for summoning's.

- Chalice- More of a symbolic piece, the Chalice is often used to hold wine or water, or for the Cakes and Ale ceremony, and symbolizes the womb of The Goddess. The Chalice embodies the Element of Water.

- Candles- Candles on a Wiccan altar represent the Goddess, God, and the Elements as well at times.

- Book of Shadows- Your Book of Shadows is where you will record your rituals, spells, insights and results. While many Wiccans keep their Book of Shadows on their altar, others simply keep it close at hand, leaving the altar uncluttered, with more room for the working of the ritual.

A great many other tools are used in Wiccan rituals: incense, besoms, bolines and cauldrons, to name just a few and all have their different functions. As you progress on your path as a Wiccan practitioner, you will discover more about these and others, as well as which ones work best for you. All ritual tools should be consecrated or blessed after being cleansed and purified when you acquire them, as well as in between rituals and uses. This prevents any unwanted energies from building up within your tools and interfering with your purposes for using them.

Placement of the items on your altar depends on the season, occasion, and preferences, but there are some simple guidelines a novice Wiccan can use to get started. Before placing your items and tools, consider the size of your altar. It doesn't really matter how elaborate or basic your set up is, as long as you have a comfortable amount of room to perform your energy work, the goal here is to provide a comfortable and functional workspace that is also personalized for you. Many Wiccans prefer to divide the altar space in half, one side devoted to the Goddess and her Elements of Water and Earth, often on the left half, and the other side for the Horned One, Air and Fire, on the right side. To represent the Gods on your altar, candles in the appropriate colors can be used. Statues or icons that symbolize the Gods for you can also be placed here. These items are often placed along with any tools or any other sacred items that are specifically representative of the Divinities, or of special meaning to you. There are most often other items, such as any offerings, personal decorations, and seasonal items, like fresh flowers for a Spring Sabbat. Some altars are also set up or aligned to honor the elements themselves, and their corresponding compass points. It is easy at this point for the novice Wiccan to become discouraged or intimidated by the sheer amount of information and tools presented already, or perhaps they might feel as though their altar needs to be an elaborate masterpiece with a devoted room in their home. While these things may certainly be desirable, Wicca instead focuses on the Intent behind the ritual, and your Spiritual journey. Your altar can be as ornate or simplified as you wish, whether the altar you choose is a solid oaken table decorated at each cross-quarter Sabbat, a small shrine that can be packed away in a suitcase for storage under the bed, or even a large flat stone beside a babbling brook. Many Wiccans keep multiple alters, as well, each for a specific purpose, such as honoring their ancestors, or a seasonal altar which they decorate according to the turning of the Wheel of the Year. Regardless of which type of alter you create, or how it is set up, a photograph or diagram in your Book of Shadows of your altar set-up is a valuable piece of information to have for later reference.

The athame was originally a ritual tool used by the Hermetic Order of the Golden Dawn for banishing rituals. It was later adapted into a broader functionality by various religious orders, including Wicca. An athame can be either single or double-edged, and conventionally has a black handle decorated according to spiritual traditions and preference. It is one of four ceremonial tools used to represent the Elements in ritual. Athames normally represent either Air or Fire, depending on spiritual Tradition, as well as intuitive choice. The athame is never used to physically cut, instead, being used to direct and channel energies, such as the ritual casting of a sacred circle. This ritual knife is also used to trace magical symbols, for invocations and evocations, and as the male symbolic element in conjunction with the feminine chalice or cauldron to represent fertility, union, and procreation.

The pentagram is an upright, five-pointed star representing the Elements and their connectedness, this symbol is often inscribed on a disk and enclosed within a circle, referred to as a pentacle (**penta**gram+ cir**cle**), these two symbols are used in a majority of Wiccan traditions, representing the Five Elements, a sacred space, the human body, and other objects and concepts. The pentacle disc, or paten, represents the Element of Earth and also is representative of the Goddess. The paten is often used for consecration, cleansing and charging other ritual tools and items, as well as being a warding, protective tool, and is also used in invocations. Wiccans often make their paten discs by inscribing, carving or painting the symbol of their Faith onto a wooden disc, or ceramic plate for use in rituals.

A wand is the ritual tool that typically represents Air or Fire, depending on which one your athame is not. The wand is a masculine tool and symbolizes the virility of The God. Wands can be made from any natural materials, most often wood, but also stone, metal or ivory are possible. These tools are normally less than a foot in length, and many are set with gems, stones, and/or inscribed with magical symbols. The wand is used to direct energies in a more gentle and passive fashion than your athame and is most often used in tracing magical symbols, sacred circles, and invoking the God and Goddess. A good training exercise for the novice Wiccan is to harvest your own wand. Finding the right fallen branch is optimal, but if you must cut yours, make certain to make an effort to connect to the tree and its Spirit energy, as you ask for its permission to take your cutting. Wait until you feel a positive response, often in the form of a sense of rightness about what you have asked and thank the tree for its gift to you. It is also a good idea to leave an offering of thanks in return. The wand is often used for summoning's that a steel or iron athame is unsuitable for.

The chalice is a symbol of Fertility and Abundance, representing the element of Water and its connection with the Mother-goddess. Chalices can be made from metal (often considered the most traditional choice) wood, ceramic or glass, and is often colored silver, a color sacred to the Goddess. Also called the goblet or simply the cup, this ritual tool has multiple functions in ritual magic such as offerings to the Divinities, as a communal libation cup like in the cakes and ale ceremony, and as a symbol representative of the womb of the Goddess, from which all Life is born. It is always prudent to be aware of any possible corrosive or unsafe reactions a liquid can induce in your chalice. If necessary, a separate libations cup should be used, and herbal teas, juice or water can always be used instead of any alcoholic beverages if you would prefer not to consume an intoxicant.

Consecrated candles are often used on an altar as representative of the God and Goddess, as well as to symbolize the elements of Earth, Air, Fire and Water, and their corresponding directions. There can be either one or two candles representing the Divinities, and of course the four for the Quarters. Candles are used in consecration, cleansings, meditational work, and as a bolster, or to positively influence some energies during a ritual. Often used during spell work, they even have their own branch of magic. Candle magic makes use of a combination of candle meditation, Herbalism, and color symbolism for energy manipulation. Many beginning Wiccans get their start with candle magic, seeing it as a non-threatening, more passive Craft.

Incense is often a symbol of Air, although it also has associations with Fire, and is often used in conjunction with a censer or cauldron while burning. Incense sticks and cones are a reasonable alternative if one does not have the means for loose incense burning. Often used as a tool for the cleansing and purifying processes, incense is also widely used in Scrying and Divination, as a meditational aid, and as an offering for rituals. Incense is a versatile tool because you can tailor your fragrances to the ritual you are performing. People with respiratory issues can easily substitute essential oils, candles or a combination of both for the same effects. Always be careful when using any incense or burning herbs that produce a cloud of smoke when there are small children or animals present, smoke inhalation can be dangerous or even deadly to some creatures such as lizards or birds.

Besoms are ceremonial brooms made of sticks or twigs secured onto a larger, central pole or staff. The besom is a traditional Wiccan fertility symbol, used to ward against negativity in many ways. Besoms are utilized to "sweep" away negativity after the birth of a child or during rituals, as a ward against bad dreams and hex magic, to cleanse and purify a ritual space, or to be joyously leapt over by a newly married couple. The besom, or Witch's Broom, is a much loved and valuable magical tool.

A Boline is a ceremonial knife, traditionally crescent shaped, used to do any ritual cutting, unlike the athame. While the crescent blade of a boline makes it ideal for harvesting herbs, many Wiccans have adopted a straighter, single-edged blade, to more practically fulfil a ritualistic purpose.

In Wiccan traditions, the Cauldron most often serves to symbolize the Water Element, The Goddess, Fertility, Change and mutability. While not considered an essential magical tool, the cauldron is nevertheless, a versatile and useful one. Some of the many uses for cauldrons are to hold ingredients and components for spell casting in readiness, to brew potions, either symbolically or actually, although you will want to check if you are using your cauldron in this way to make sure that it is a food-safe material, some store-bought cauldrons contain lead, and shouldn't be used for anything that is to be consumed. The cauldron is also used for scrying and divinatory means, and as a safe place for any burning ritual components, such as incense or candles to extinguish safely.

Witchcraft starts with research, it involves learning more about the path you've chosen and its history, practices and evolution. You're off to a great start since you've already read this far, but don't stop here! Most Wiccans are continuously researching and expanding their knowledge of Wicca, Magic and Witchcraft, Nature and the Divinities. This research allows them to further their knowledge, and confidently put it into practice through experimentation. That being said, nobody wants a mechanic to work on their car if that mechanic has only read manuals and books on the subject of cars! The next step on the Wiccan Path is experimentation. This means taking all the knowledge you've gained from your research, and finding out what works best for you, as an individual. To do this, one can meditate, walk-in natural settings to and learn and identify the elements of Nature, speak to any other Wiccans you may come across, either online or in-person, and of course, read and research, so that you can gain confidence in your abilities and skills and start to put into practice the things you learn.

While the source for energy is the Five Elements, and the basis for energetic manipulation is ritual, by learning the basic steps of a ritual, you are training yourself for manipulating energies. This is how you begin to "learn magic". Some steps, techniques and advice are given as a way to get the reader started on their Wiccan journey, but this shouldn't be taken as definitive either in process or structure. A Wiccan practitioner's path is one of self-discovery and finding your method and own insights is a large part of Wicca. One's approach to magic should be as comfortable, confident and earnest as possible. Record your insights, experiences and revelations in your Book of Shadows, so you may look back through it as a record of your journey, and keep it as a working, evolving companion on your Path of Spirituality.

Chapter 6: The Wiccan Book of Shadows

A Book of Shadows is a book containing religious text, rituals, spells and magical wisdom. Wiccans who keep a Book of Shadows (BoS) do so to have a record of their spiritual and magical experiences. Grimoires like these provide reference points from which a practitioner of Wicca can easily gain access to all of their past experiences and gathered knowledge that has been accumulated along their spiritual, religious, and magical journey. A BoS contains not only spiritual text but also instructions used for rituals and spell casting.

The original of the Book of Shadows is unknown, as this is a tradition that witches and covens have honored throughout the history of the craft. The most famous or well-known was created by Gerald Gardner with collaboration from Doreen Valiente, his High Priestess at the time, for use in his Bricket Wood coven. Many witches who practice some of the British Traditional branches of Wicca, still use a form of this Book of Shadows, having been passed down from Gardner's initiates with a few alterations and additions made along the way. Gardner's original text was a closely guarded secret, with jumbled instructions and antiquated writing styles used to confuse the uninitiated reader. Gardner claimed much of this was historical in origin, having been passed down orally from the era that witches were prosecuted and tortured, although the contents of which have been made public and even published several times since his death. Although many of his claims about his sources have been disputed, those Gardnerians still using his BoS have since added to it and adapted some of its rituals and teachings, but have never removed content.

Members of some covens occasionally even use two Books of Shadows (BsoS), one being a set of core practices, rituals and spells for use when the coven gathers, and the other being copied by a novice from the coven's BoS as a start for their personal version. There are even familial grimoires that have been passed down to a witch's descendants, heirlooms of historical texts containing advice, family traditions, and lore exclusive to that ancestry. Whether it is a day-by-day recording of a Wiccan's spiritual journey, a "recipe book" of spells, components and ritual instructions, an accounting of ritualistic practices of a coven, or even an electronic file created on a hard drive, a BoS is a highly personal and intuitive magical tool. What is important for a novice Wiccan to remember, is that a BoS may start small, but will expand over the years with your growing knowledge as you add to it. Because a BoS is a personal recording of your spiritual journey, there are no real guidelines or strict rules about what should be in one. While one person may record every step of a ritual, fastidiously noting every word, candle placement and phase of the moon, another might simply write down the intent of a ritual, what spells if any, were cast, and what the results were. In spite of there being no "wrong" or "right" way to keep your BoS, there are still some things that will make it easier for the novice to fashion their grimoire.

The first step to creating your Book of Shadows is to get a book that will be suitable for the purpose you intend. This can be anything from a composition notebook, a blank diary, or a leather-bound tome, meant to last for generations. The choice is yours to make, however, try not to get too caught up in how your BoS will look for right now, you can always add to it, or copy what you have into another Book at any time. In all honesty, many Wiccans prefer to use, and highly recommend using a three-ring binder for their BoS! Don't be too surprised, using a binder like this allows you to easily add, subtract and reorder your BoS. An additional benefit to using a binder is that because they are normally utilitarian and plain on the outside, they can be decorated in any way the user wishes. Once you have your BoS, make sure you cleanse and consecrate it like you would any of your magical tools, it might just become the most important one in your repertoire.

There are so many possibilities for your own Book of Shadows, that it's easy to feel overloaded with information. A good rule of thumb for adding new information into your BoS is to ask yourself if the item is something you feel is relevant and valuable enough to your spiritual path to be included. You needn't try to "finish" your BoS, it should be an evolving, changeable item because it will mirror your spiritual growth. One more tip for the beginning Wiccan is to remember to record your sources. This will ensure that you can re-reference them if needed, and also carries the benefit of allowing you to ask permission of the author of your material if you ever wish to share your information in any public forum.

Now it's time to create a title page for your Book of Shadows. The Title Page for your BoS should include at the very least, your name, and commonly, some sort of description as well, such as, "This is the Book of Shadows of Jane Doe". A blessing, statement of intent, dedication or inscription can be included if desired, as well. The Title page can be as simple or ornate as you want it to be, just as long as it is special to you personally.

The next step for your Book of Shadows is to decide how you'll want to organize it. There are many different ways to organize your BoS, but three of the more popular ways to do this are by utilizing either an Index, Tab, or Table of Contents organization style. When using the Index method, the main topics in your BoS are listed somewhere near the front or back of the Book. When you add to your BoS or write a new entry, list the page number used under the appropriate topic in the Index. This method gives you a listing of all pages the topic you are searching for is referenced on. When using the Tab method, your BoS is organized by dividing it into sections, how many is up to you depending on what you want in your BoS and delineating each section with a Tab so that it is easily identified. This method works best when used with a binder, so that the sections can be easily changed or moved, but can be adapted for use in a bound BoS. Using a Table of Contents is much the same as the Tab method, only rather than using Tabs, your different sections will have page numbers for the starting point of each Topic.

One final method of organizing your BoS is to do it digitally. Wicca is an evolving, constantly changing spirituality, both in nature, as well as for its followers. There isn't any real reason that a witch can't keep their BoS stored electronically. In the times we live in, with work pressures, appointments to keep, busy lifestyles, tiny houses, cloud storage, and phone apps, you may decide to keep your BoS on a computer file or hard drive. When you create your BoS this way you have the advantage of everything right there at your fingertips. Websites are far easier to save and re-access later, and you can move your categories around under the main folder even easier than someone working with a Tabs or Categories method. There are even ways to store your BoS digitally and access it from your phone, or work computer, so the witch- on-the-go never has to be without their grimoire. One drawback to this method, however, is that you must normally scan everything into your computer first, before using the information. This is normally not much of a problem, and indeed Wiccans who use this method expound on its virtues. Another possibility when using this method is the lack of a power source. If you store you BoS digitally and lose the power to your electronic device you save it on, the information could be lost, or you may not be able to see your BoS if you "run out of juice"!

Now that you have your Book of Shadows started, you will need to decide what information to record in it. While the data you accumulate in your BoS should be specific to you and your spiritual journey, some items generally make a BoS into an invaluable personal reference guide for Wicca. Some commonalities found in a great many BsoS:

- Religious information- Beliefs, morals, ethics, information on specific Wiccan Tradition you follow, chosen deities, theology.

- Rituals and Ceremonies- Structure, tools, procedures, Sabbats, Esbats, Holy Days.

- Tables and Correspondences- Charts, symbols, glyphs, lists.

- Spells- Components, results, notes, dates and times.

- Chants, Prayers, and Songs- recitations, poems, invocations not included in Rituals category.

- Reading- Sources of information, references, books, websites.

- Journal- Personal insights.

A section on Religious Information could include copies of the Long Rede, a listing of the Thirteen Principles, The Law of Three or any insights you have on your spiritual path as a Wiccan. If you want to incorporate pieces of another Tradition or religion, like the Norse Nine Noble Virtues, into your Wiccan Path, this is a good place for it. Many witches include information on their specific Tradition of Wicca if they follow one, and their chosen Deities or Gods. This section of your BoS would also be a good place to record information about any specific ideologies of your coven.

The Rituals and Ceremonies category in a Book of Shadows tends to include information on the Sabbats, Esbats, or any Holy Days you observe. Any rituals you perform or are a participant of, are recorded here. Make sure you include times, dates, and any readings, or chants that were recited. Include the exact steps you took and anything that seemed particularly interesting about your results. Unless you performed your ritual alone, it is a good idea to record any other participants here as well. Later on, this can tell you whose energies work well with yours, and for what specific purposes. This chapter of your BoS is where you will turn to time and again, perhaps because you are always too busy to remember the entire Yule poem you like to recite on the Winter Solstice, or to get the details of the ritual you worked three years ago, for instance, that you felt was an incredible success afterwards, so you can repeat it. It will also be where you remind yourself to not use that brand of incense for the next Candlemas, and that it's not a great idea to use a certain spell during Samhain. The Rituals and Ceremonies section of your BoS will be a rich, and personalized wealth of information for how you perform Your Craft.

A section on charts, sigils, correspondences, and other items of a symbolic nature are found in most Books of Shadows, these could include anything from sigils or symbols you find important, a diagram of the Elemental Pentagram with the Directions and candle colors that accompany them, a listing of the herbs used for healing, Runic correspondences for the I-Ching, to gemstone and birthday equivalents for the Zodiac. The amount of data you will probably keep stored in this chapter is vast, so leave a good amount of room if you are using the Tabs or Table of Contents method to organize your Book.

Of course, no Book of Shadows would be complete without a category for Spell work. This part of your BoS will be one of the most dynamic because the information you collect here will grow, change and adapt as much as you do on your spiritual journey. Often included in this section will be data such as the name of the spell you work, the components, results, and your thoughts, including anything that felt "off" or components you might have changed. Additions to spells are often added in later, after the spell-work is done, sometimes even after the results have manifested themselves. Unlike your Rituals section, you won't need to be so specific about the steps of the ritual itself, unless it has some bearing on the actual spell. What you should focus on for this chapter of your grimoire are the intricate details of each particular spell. You should include information such as if it is a time-sensitive or divinatory spell, or if it should be performed at a specific time of year. Any spell components should be listed here in detail. What color candles were used, any herbs, and make sure you specify whether they were freshly cut, dried or burned. Include details on what you thought about the results of the spell, if you thought that it worked the way it was supposed to, and anything you think you would change or remove from the process. Go into as much detail as possible for this chapter, it will be like a "cookbook" for you as a practicing Wiccan.

Many Books of Shadows have a separate category for chants, prayers and elements of that nature, where you can include the passages that are the most significant to you. These can be a mantra you say every morning, the mealtime prayer your grandmother used to say, or a beautiful chant you heard at the last Sabbat. Be sure to include the name of the author if you are able so that you can credit their work. These passages don't necessarily have to be in a ritual or part of a spell, they just need to be significant to you. Many witches will write the lines of The Drawing Down the Moon ritual here as well as in their Rituals section, just because it's a beautiful poem or the lyrics to a song they remember from their childhood simply because it still resonates with them. You can even get creative and devise your poetry, or chants for this section, then try some out in a ritual.

Many Wiccans also provide a Preferred Reading category in their grimoires. This chapter would include entries such as websites, newsletters, and books you often use for research and information gathering. Taking clear, thorough notes in this section will help you later on if you need to cite a source, gather more information, or cross-reference some data. This is a Chapter you will want to update regularly. Websites close down, and books are added to collections, make certain to note any changes in your literature and research sources to avoid frustrating, wasted time later on.

Near the end of most Books of Shadows, you will often find a personal diary or Journal section. This is the part of your BoS where you should write down your own thoughts, inspirations, questions, answers, old scraps of poetry that you love, or the address of that really good incense shop, anything that seems relevant to you , but may not have a place in the other categories of your BoS. This section will also contain more of your personality and energies. Write down your dreams, if you wish here, or keep an entirely separate chapter just for that. Of course, it's optimal if you record in your journal section every day, but we all know that Life often interferes with our plans. Try to record in your Journal chapter as much as you possibly can, and eventually, it will come easier (and more frequently) to you. Times to add entries to this section would be if you receive any omens or flashes if insight, record what it was, the date and as much as you can remember about the situation. When you meet new people that are practicing Wicca jot down their names and your first impressions (and you won't forget their names later if you see them again).

Chapter 7: First Steps for A Novice-How to Start on Your Personal Wiccan Path

The first step on a Wiccan spiritual journey is to study. Learn all you can about Wicca in general. You've already started, so keep up the good work! Research the Gods, Goddesses, ethos and different Traditions of Wicca. Find out how you resonate with the individual Elements or seasons. Learn all you can about Wiccan rituals, the Sabbats and Esbats, and why ritual and magic are so central in Wicca. As you progress in your knowledge, you'll begin to feel connections with or affinities to particular deities or elements, or certain tenets that seem to be just what you need.

If you find yourself curious about a certain Tradition, track down everything you possibly can, to see what it is that interests you. Take notes and keep track of information that seems more relevant to you especially. Record your opinions on aspects of Wicca, different Traditions, the allure of working with a coven to you, or which Gods or Goddess you feel drawn to. Since Wicca is an exploratory spirituality, with no overall hard directives, it is left to the individual to choose which aspects of it they fit into, and those that are right for them. The Long Rede and Law of Three are ethical "codes of conduct" that Wiccans live by, but they are merely guidelines to work within, how you do so is always your own choice. If you feel drawn to the Goddess of the Dianic Tradition, but the ritual style of the shamans of North America, then you should study the Eclectic Tradition, and perhaps make your own blending of Wicca. You will want to become familiar with the seasons and cycles of the earth, which rituals are held when, and so much more. You will soon discover that Wicca is a rich, vibrant and evolvable spiritual journey shaped by the practitioner along their way.

Take time in your research, there is no hurry! The most important "schedule" in Wicca is the Wheel of the Year, and you don't have to accomplish anything on a timeline. While it is a widely accepted tradition that an initiate of Wicca will study for a year and one day before dedicating themselves to the Craft, you can take as long as you need. The length of time you have been researching your spirituality choice is far less important than the knowledge you gain from it. The Wiccan faith holds each individual practitioner responsible for their actions and choices. If you feel after six months of study that you have enough of a grasp on the Tradition that interests you, then you may be ready for a self-dedication, if you study for longer, just to get a handle on information that is coming slowly for you, that's completely ok, too. Most Wiccans won't tell you that you absolutely must do things in a certain way, or in an arbitrary timeframe, that's just not what Wicca is about. As long as you try to live a moral, ethical lifestyle, uphold your chosen Deities, and honor the Earth, her cycles and Nature, you are already following a Wiccan path.

Once you've chosen your Deities, Tradition, and feel comfortable as a practicing Wiccan, it's time to start thinking more about rituals. Ritual is a very large, and important part of the Wiccan spirituality. If you are fortunate enough to have a mentor or friends who are also Wiccan, ask what works best for them, they can be a valuable asset. If you are a solitary practitioner, simply go back to your studies. Learn the steps to cleanse and purify, how to cast a Sacred Circle and how to close one. Find out which rituals to perform for the Sabbats, and Esbats, and the differences between each. One could say that two of the most important tools a Wiccan uses are Knowledge and Reason. It would be both illogical and irresponsible to invoke a Deity you know nothing about or cast a spell without first learning about any possible ramifications, so be responsible and logical in your experimentation. Research every aspect of the ritual you are building, and logically piece it together. Your research will often show you that there are plenty of others who have trod the same path, and most of the time, they are very happy to share their experience. Don't be afraid to use something just because you didn't come up with it on your own. Use what works best, even if it isn't original, it's what's "tried and true"! When you are comfortable enough that you know the building blocks of a basic ritual, try to create your own. Many novices perform a Self-Dedication ritual for their first try. Your ritual doesn't have to be fancy or elaborate, as long as it reflects what you feel are the most important aspects of your chosen tradition. Rituals can be large, small, simple or complicated, as long as they include what is important to you. Write down the steps of your first ritual, knowing that it is likely to grow and evolve, just as you do on your spiritual journey. You can take your time: a ritual doesn't have to be manufactured in a single evening. You should put as much reflection into creating your ritual as you did in choosing your Gods and your Spiritual path. Make sure to study your ritual, and that you know all the steps and components, so that it will become almost second nature to you, and your ritual will go smoothly, without missteps.

Now that you have a solid grasp on Wicca, and how your ritual will work, it's time to start practicing. Many novices at this point will wish to jump straight into performing rituals right away. While this isn't necessarily "wrong", it can lead to confusion and dissatisfaction later, if you haven't fully grasped all the nuances that go into your ritual. A good way to be sure about your process and find out what your inner voice is telling you, is meditation. Meditation can help us connect with the energies within ourselves as well as those flowing around us. It is the first step you will take to gain mental discipline, which is a necessary component in performing rituals, and casting spells, and it will help you along your chosen path as well as in your everyday life, by increasing focus and mental clarity. Two types of meditation are an essential part of Wicca and magic, passive meditation, and what some call active meditation, although this term is used loosely, and varies in meaning. It is easier to become adept at active meditation once you have mastered passive meditation.

Passive meditation is the art of relaxing the body and clearing the mind. We often go through our daily routines as a victim of multiple stressors in our lives, from waking up with a sore neck, disagreeing with a co-worker, to worrying about how to tell someone how you feel about them. In passive meditation, your goal will be to release, and get rid of these stressors, so that your mind can reach a relaxed, and clear state of existence. This mental "clearing" is the basis of focusing your intent during the ritual, as well as listening to your inner voice and gaining knowledge from the insights provided. During this meditation, the individual seeks to consciously relax and calm the body, mind and emotions. There are many ways to get into a passive meditational state, and you should try out as many as you like, see which ones work best for you. One method to achieve passive meditation is to "teach" your body how to relax on all levels. First, choose your spot. Many Wiccans enjoy meditating in Nature, to better feel the Elements, and the earth's rhythms, but if inclement weather prevents this, in front of your alter is a good spot, as is any quiet, not-overly- bright room. Anywhere you feel comfortable, relaxed, and safe is ideal. It's also a good idea to turn off your phone and make certain no unwanted interruptions will occur during your meditating. Find a spot that is not regularly visited, if you decide to practice outdoors, or just dim the lights, make sure the thermostat is at a comfortable temperature, use the restroom, and make sure no distractions will interrupt your exercise. Next, sit comfortably, it is recommended to sit with your back straight, and arms and legs unfolded, but if the classic Lotus position is what makes you relaxed, go for it. It's generally not a good idea to lie down or be so comfortable that you fall asleep when you reach your relaxed state, however! If you do fall asleep, many people do, don't worry, just start over and try again, meditation can't be "overdone".

When you are comfortable, take a few deep breaths, as you picture your breathing, imagine your breath clearing away the outside world like the winds push the clouds, and start to focus on your inner being. Start by calming yourself and relaxing your body. To accomplish this, focus your attention inward and downward, concentrating on your feet and toes. Tell these parts of yourself to be calm and relaxed. You can hold an internal conversation with each part of your body as you gradually move upward, through your legs, hips, lower and upper torso, neck and head. Tell each part of your body, as you move upward, to release those tensions, to be calm. Tell each part it is safe, and it can let go, it is now time to relax. Search out any tensions and visualize them as melting or drifting away from your body, and let them go. This will take some practice, and it is ok if you can't release all of your tensions right away, or on your first try. Meditation is a skill and needs to be practiced to be perfected, don't get discouraged, it will eventually become easier for you to achieve a relaxed state. Relaxing the body first is important, because if you skip this step, your mind and heart, your emotions, won't be able to be calmed. If you hold tension in the body, your mind will home in on that stress, and you will not be able to focus on your goal.

Once you have calmed the body, it is time to relax the mind. Calming the mind works in a similar way to calming the body but isn't quite as easy. To calm the mind, turn to your thoughts and let them come to you one at a time. Tell your mind that it has nothing to fear and that it is ok to let go of each individual thought. Let your mind know that you will keep it safe and that it is time to relax. Each thought that comes to you should be acknowledged, and let go, see it floating away, or fading from existence. Once you have your mind calmed, it should feel clear, like a deep pool of pristine water. This will help you to relax your heart, or emotions next.

Next, concentrate on your Emotions. The thoughts you calmed earlier were conscious, emotions don't always come from the same place within ourselves. If you've ever been to a beautiful place in Nature, and found yourself with tears in your eyes just for the sheer joy of being there, or decided to not walk home one night, just because you "got a bad feeling", these were examples of an unconscious emotional response. These are what you will strive to quiet next. While you focus on your emotions, realize that they may have nothing at all to do with conscious thought, but are still a distraction. Tell your heart that it is safe, and that it is ok to feel these emotions, but that it's now time to let go of negativity. Acknowledge emotions like anger and doubt, then let them go. See them moving away from you like a cloud, then disappearing. Tell your emotional being to relax.

By now your body, mind and emotions have all been "trained" to hear, and trust your inner voice, and to release the tensions within you when instructed to. When you feel all the negativity has been drained from you, and your body, mind, and emotions have been freed of those things you let go of, you have successfully cleared your mind in a meditative state. Keep practicing so this exercise becomes almost second nature to you. Meditation takes plenty of practice, but it will become much easier as you keep trying. Now that you have achieved clarity and a relaxed inner core, you can stop here if you wish, this is a very healing state, where your body and mind can "reset" and just **be**, in silence and peace, or continue to your active meditation below.

Another way to describe this exercise is "active listening." As human beings, we like to, and it can even be said that we need to, communicate. However, we often lose sight of the fact that a large part of communication is about listening. When you are with another person, most people feel a need to fill the silence because it makes them feel uncomfortable or awkward. During a conversation, it is common for a person to only listen until they feel the need or urge to reply. If a companion says to you "I had a great day" your first response is just that, a response. Your mind's immediate inclination is to formulate a response, whether it's "me too" or "how so," because your brain has sprinted ahead, and is already working to fill the gap in the conversation. However, when this happens, you're not listening to everything the other person says because you are already formulating your reply. That part of your brain that listens to people isn't functioning fully because the part that formulates speech is already trying to figure out what to say. This isn't necessarily "wrong", it's just how people tend to work. When you practice active listening as you meditate, you are training your mind to listen instead of responding.

Once you have stilled the tensions in your body and let your mind relax, you will be more open, and can better sense the energies flowing within and around you. At this point in your meditation, you should be able to let thoughts or images arise in your mind. Let them come one at a time so that you can examine each one, in turn, to learn where it originates from, and it's an influence on you. (As a side note, many Wiccans receive their Deity calling in this meditative state.) Concentrate on the image your mind has pulled into your consciousness, whether that image is a pentacle, the ocean, or the neighbor's housecat. Let your Lower, or subconscious speak to you and don't respond, just listen. These images are what your subconscious mind has decided to reveal to you now that you can "hear" them clearly. Don't worry if you don't understand the image, just keep at it, and allow yourself to concentrate fully on that one image. If you are persistent, you will eventually come to understand what your mind is telling you, and the connections between you and the image in your mind. If you see a pentacle, study it, try to feel the energy contained within the symbol while you allow yourself to become absorbed in it, soon enough, you'll begin to receive insights and ideas about this symbol that you never realized were within you. If it's the neighbor's cat, do the same, can you feel the fur, or hear the cat meowing? You may eventually come to realize that this cat is always there at the window when you leave every morning, and you just didn't realize that it was the reason you smile on your way to work. Meditation like this is a good way to improve your focus and learn more about the energies within you, and those that interact with you from without, as well.

Now that you can clear your mind, and hold focus on an image or concept, it's time to consciously guide your meditation. This is very similar to the first two exercises, only instead of letting an image or thought come randomly, you will choose the object of focus yourself. Begin meditation as you normally would, let your body, mind, and emotions relax and clear. When you have slowed your mind enough to reach a relaxed state think about your object of focus, if it's small enough, like a stone, for example, you can also hold it. A symbol can also be used to represent a concept to make it easier to focus on. For instance, if you decide to meditate on the Five Elements, you may wish to use a pentagram to represent the concept of them and how they fit together. Hold this image in your mind so that you can observe it from every level and perspective. Now imagine that you can experience this object with all of your senses. How does it taste? What does it sound like, and how does it smell? When you feel yourself losing focus, or you may simply feel "done" with your exercise, let yourself return slowly to awareness of the world around you. This may take a few sessions to get right, or to simply get all the answers your subconscious is trying to give to you, but, once again, with practice, it will come to you. Some Wiccans like to offer a prayer, or say a blessing at the end of their meditations. This isn't necessary but can often add a sense of closure to your sessions. Once you have finished, you may want to jot down some notes, or any particularly strong impressions. Meditation takes practice, and is not instantaneous, try not to get frustrated if you need to start over. Remember, the benefits will be more than worth the effort!

Cleansing and purifying energy is a simple and easy way for the novice Wiccan to practice Focus and Intent. Because cleansing an object is a relatively passive act without the added pressure of a full-blown ritual, as long as you remain focused on your intent, cleansing can't be overdone or done in a "wrong" way. The act of cleansing an object is a gentle clearing away of any negative energies. Unlike Banishing, which is a forceful ejection, Cleansing is merely letting any negative energies in a person, place, or object let go and fall away, to be turned into neutral energy or to simply disappear. One approach to focusing on your intent to cleanse is to visualize all the negative energies in the object of the cleansing as lifting away and exiting the object or see it in your mind's eye as changing into positive, beneficial energy. First, choose what needs to be cleansed, perhaps you just got a new Athame, maybe your house has had a heavy, cluttered feel to it recently, or perhaps you've just been feeling overly tired, and bogged down with negativity lately. Once you've chosen what needs to be Purified, pick which method of Purification that will work best.
Some Purification/Cleansing techniques are:

- Smoke cleansing, sometimes called smudging, is commonly done with herb bundles, bits of wood or incense that produces a purifying smoke. Also called recaning, smoke cleansing is one of the most widely used purification rituals performed. Some items used for recaning are sage, cedar, Palo Santo wood and specially blended incense. This form of cleansing is very simple to perform, but can sometimes be a poor choice if small animals, children, or other forms of wildlife are present, as it can be damaging to the lungs and disrupt breathing. First, light the herbs that you'll be recaning with, and then allow them to smolder. Remember, the object here is to Cleanse with the smoke, so you don't want an actual flame. Allow the smoke to drift over the object to be cleansed, fanning it with your hand, or a feather, and visualize the negativity loosening its ties to the object, and floating away and becoming neutral, then disappearing.

- Sun and moonlight are also wonderful, and perhaps the easiest cleansing tools at the Wiccan's fingertips! When purifying with sun or moonlight, simply place your object in the direct rays of the sun or full moon, the time varies but is generally no longer than a few hours or overnight. You can say words of blessing over the object or state your intent to have it cleared of negativity before leaving it. If you are using the full moon, it's a good idea to leave it overnight. Retrieve the item afterwards, and either say a blessing or give thanks to the elements for their help, and your item is ready to be charged. This technique works especially well for crystals and gemstones.

- Purification with water is also, a common method used. Washing or soaking an object in purified water is a much-used practice, as is ritual bathing, either in private or out in nature under a full moon. You can cleanse an object just by submerging it in the ocean, or if you are not near a coast, try a running source of water, like a stream or river. Bear in mind that some objects become harmful, toxic, or damaged when submerged, so choose this technique for items that can be safely introduced to water. For cleansing water, you should take your bowl of water, and leave it under the full moon or sunlight for a few hours, or overnight if it's moonlight you are using. It is best if you can to use a bowl made from glass, but you can use wood or ceramic, just make sure that the bowl you're using isn't plastic, as it isn't a natural material. The water to be purified should be natural, so try for spring water, or just filter the water you use beforehand. It is also optimal to place your cleansing water in direct moonlight or sun, but this isn't necessary if you leave the water there longer. As you place your water, state your intent to purify it, you can even say some words of prayer or blessings. When you retrieve your water, it will be ready to use for cleansing, either by immersing your object in the bowl or by dipping your fingers into it and lightly sprinkling the object to be cleansed. At this point, you can add a prayer or blessing over the water to consecrate it if you wish. This method can also be used for salt-water cleansing. Before you place your bowl of water, just add natural, or sea salt to it, and proceed the same way. Remember to be careful if you are using saltwater because it can be corrosive and damaging to metal, leather, some crystals and other materials, such as fabrics. Another way to water cleanse an object is to leave it out in the rain, light spring rain is best, however, just make sure that your object won't be damaged by winds, or washed away.

- When Choosing burial for cleansing, simply bury your object in salt for twelve to twenty-four hours. Say a prayer or blessing as you bury your object, or state your intent, and your item will be cleansed when you remove it. For soil burial, plant your object in the ground, as you state your intent to have all negative energies removed, and leave it for up to a week, for the best results leave your item close to a seedling of some sort. A handy tip for soil or salt burial cleansing is to use a bowl or pot so your item is easily retrieved, or you can mark the location by using a flag or some other indicator of where you buried it.

- Another method of ritual cleansing is sound. In this case, purification is achieved by using drums, bells, the voice, in the form of chanting or singing, or any number of items that can make the sound desired. Many Wiccans simply use the sound of clapping their hands together sharply. Sound cleansing is an excellent choice for fragile or delicate items and can be done nearly anywhere. When you have decided which object to cleanse, use your cleansing purification tool, in this example we'll use a bell, to make the desired noise all around the object. Some practitioners also chant a blessing or purification mantra as they do this. Visualize all the unwanted energies being broken up by the sound and dissolving away as you do this. When you are satisfied, either charge the object with new positive energy or place a ward to prevent any undesirable energy from returning.

- Crystals are also commonly used in ritual cleansings. When purification is done with crystals, be sure to choose one that releases energy, instead of retaining it. Two good examples are citrine and smoky quartz. You can also just cleanse the crystal itself after you use it to purify an object. Start with a cleansed crystal, aside from smoky quartz and citrine, black tourmaline, and amethyst make excellent options, too. Hold your crystal up as you ask the Elements or the Divine to help you remove unwanted energy, state your intent of having the crystal absorb all the negativity and clear the object, then thank the Elements or Divinities for their aid. Once you are finished, it's a good idea to cleanse the crystal itself, so that you can use it again another time. Think of this last step the same way you would go about cleaning a counter, in that you wouldn't use the same sponge you just wiped the dirt away with before rinsing it out.

- Using a besom to cleanse is another very easy, and perhaps one of the most traditional ways to cleanse. Besoms can be used in all manner of ways during a ritual, but one of the most common is cleansing away unwanted energies. This cleansing method works extremely well for rooms, or very large spaces, and is often used specifically to purify an area before casting a magic circle. To perform a besom cleanse, simply state your intent or chant a mantra of cleansing while you perform a sweeping motion with your besom. Many practitioners of The Craft prefer to sweep from West to East, but your intent is what is the most important. As you "sweep" the negativity away, see all the undesirable energies being brushed out of the way. Let them disappear with the dust of the cleansing. A besom cleansing is often done at the time of Spring cleaning to start the new year off fortuitously.

Centering and grounding are techniques used to improve focus and get rid of excess, or negative energy. Centering is the act of finding a harmonious balance within one's self, and is a skill that may take some practice to master but is entirely worth the effort. Like meditation, Centering helps us get "back in touch" or in tune with what is going on with our internal energies. This allows us to put things going on in our lives into perspective, grow more in our spirituality, and balance our emotions and thoughts. If an individual is not centered properly, they can often seem unfocused, forgetful, overwhelmed, emotional or just restless. Centering techniques are similar to meditation, they involve visualizing a consolidation of your energy, and a pulling back of those energies that you have scattered elsewhere, like work, and other stresses. Once this is accomplished, the energy is then focused towards your goals or the intent of a ritual. Centering is often done at the beginning of a ritual as a means of creating more focus on the intent. If you practice meditation, try adding Centering to your meditation session. Once you have reached the state where your mind, body and emotions are clear, visualize your energies as ribbons, or strands that reach out to all of our energetic connections. Now imagine pulling those ribbons back in, so that you are not so energetically "spread out". Centering helps you to make better choices about where to invest your energies.

Now that you have all the basics down, it is finally time to go forth and practice! Once you feel comfortable with Meditation to focus your intent, and cleansing, grounding and centering, it's a good time to try and put some of your new-found knowledge to work. This is when you should put all the steps together to practice your chosen Craft. Of course, practice *is* the operative word, witchcraft isn't perfected overnight. Don't worry if you get off to a slow start, can't quite come up with a good chant to Call the Quarters, or work a spell that just fizzles. Know that the intent behind your actions is what is important, and as long as you try to stay true to the Wiccan path and the things it stands for, such as the Law of Three and the Long Rede, you won't go wrong. Scientists experiment in their chosen fields because they wish to see what the end results are. They are doing scientifically what a witch does with energy and spell workings. Witchcraft takes practice and experimentation before you know what results will come from some of your actions. We've all seen the cliché movies and television shows where a witch casts a spell that goes "horribly wrong" and of course, the protagonist must then save the witch, themselves, or the world! If you know your intent and focus on what you are doing during a ritual or spell casting, this won't happen. The most that can usually go "horribly wrong" during a ritual or casting is a distraction that disrupts the energies of the working. This means that you simply need to start over, and perhaps rethink your steps. In most cases, the only thing you'll end up losing is time. Often the Gods will send a disruption to let you know that the ritual or spell you cast is not what you need, or that it just isn't the right time. When your energy workings don't go the way you want, pay attention to why it happened that way, instead of getting frustrated. Wiccans are in tune with the Divinities and Elements like very few people who do not practice witchcraft are, and because of this, can hear the "messages" from the Gods, higher and lower consciousnesses, and the very Elemental spirits of Nature around them when others cannot.

To allow your spell casting to go more smoothly, you should also create avenues to direct your energies. If you go through all the steps to perfect a ritual, cast a sacred circle, and then your spell, but just leave it at that, chances are, your spell will not work according to the way you want it to. This is because you haven't allowed the energies of your spell to travel in a direct path to your intentions. To do this, you need to create as much room for the energies of the spell to work as possible. If you remember the example of Sally, and our healing spell, when you wrote down your intent, you were visualizing the outcome of the spell even before it was cast. You saw her in your mind's eye as being healthy, and maybe even told her husband that that tree out front could be aggravating her allergies, causing him to trim it back. This is referred to as creating a channel for your spell to work. you not only cast a spell, but you also gave that energy a positive outlet to aim for. In another example, let's say you want to cast a money spell for yourself. First, you go through the steps of your ritual, finding just the right candles, herbs, crystals and incantations for your spell. Then you cast your sacred circle, perform your ritual and cast your spell to not be in debt, and poof! you're done, right? Wrong. Creating a channel for your energetic workings is like digging an irrigation trench. You need water in a certain place, so you make the land that needs watering more accessible to the natural flow of the water. If you don't dig a trench, you most likely won't get the water your crops need. This holds true with energy as well. With our money spell above, to create a channel for the spell's energy, you must give it somewhere to flow to, just like your irrigation ditch. This could be in the form of sending out a job application, or three, or perhaps a couple of people owe you some money, try contacting them and asking if it's a good time to collect. You are much more likely to get successful results from a spell you create a channel for.

Along with creating channels for your spells, you should become aware of the effects of your mindset when performing your rituals and spell castings. A lot of this can simply be done by adjusting your language and inner dialogue. In our experimental money spell, we didn't create channels for that spell to go, but we also weren't being positive in our intent and language. Rather than saying I *don't* want to be in debt, try saying my debt will decrease and my bank account will expand. This gives the Elements and the energies you created in your spell a positive goal to achieve, rather than something to *not* aim for. The difference is subtle but quite powerful in effect, and not difficult to implement.

Another helpful tip is that casting spells are usually much more effective when the object or person of the spell is working with you. In Sally's example again, you not only worked a healing spell for her, but by giving her the crystal, and personalizing the intent of the spell, you were allowing her to help you direct the energies of the spell to your will. You even told her husband about the tree, so his energies were working in your favour, too, whether he realized it or not. Try not to cast spells (especially those of a negative sort) on people who are unaware of your intentions. This is not only normally ineffective but borders on immoral, depending on your intentions. Wiccans can be likened to the Healers in a community, and this being so, wouldn't practice their Craft on an unwilling or even unknowing subject. Respect is a thing that is given and earned, you can't take it for yourself, Magical energies work the same way in that you can only create an opportunity for your will to manifest. You won't be able to harness the Elements, let alone cast effective spells if you haven't put in the hard work on research and practice it takes to do so. If you cast negative energy out, you will get negativity back in return, so always be sure of your intentions when practicing your Craft.

Hopefully, by now you have an understanding of not just how to work magic, but how magic works, as well. Magic is not the fantasy that many works of fiction portray it to be. You most likely won't be able to materialize vast amounts of cash by casting a money spell without the hard work that goes into energy manipulation, and Sally may never be quite rid of her seasonal allergies, but you can help to alleviate some of her symptoms with spells, crystals, and even herbal teas (potions!). Working magic is exactly that, work! Without conscious effort on the part of the Wiccan, the energies that are at your disposal won't have a conduit to be directed at, and the will can't be manifested. Magic is all around us, from the growing things that fight their way to the surface to bloom every spring, to the moonlight on our faces as we give thanks to the Goddess. Magic is within the rituals, Esbats, and Elemental beings that exist all around us, as well as the stones, oceans and stars, and each person alive has it within them to be a "magical" being, not just those that follow a Wiccan path. The difference between those that work magic and those who deny its existence is awareness. Wiccans are aware of the cycles of nature and the energies flowing around and through us, every moment of every day, and have trained themselves to be able to manipulate them for the betterment of ourselves and those around us. A Wiccan mindset is key to walking through the world with a sense of wonder and learning how the Earth and the Divinities speak to us through the natural world. When we understand and recognize the energies around us, we can open ourselves up to the true magic of the Cosmos.

Chapter 8: Solitary Practice VS Covens

Now that you've started on your spiritual journey through Wicca, it's time to decide whether or not you'll be joining a coven, practicing occasionally with a Circle, or remain as a solitary practitioner. Covens are a group of Wiccans who share the same Traditions, and philosophies that practice their Craft together on a regular basis and perform rituals together. Since Wicca "jumped the pond" to North America and started to rapidly spread across the world, more and more people have welcomed this spiritual path into their lives. Many of these were initiated into The Craft by British Traditional Wiccans who brought their Traditions from England and started their own covens. Covens are often considered a familial group of Wiccans, and many who join them do so for the sense of belonging they get from this group atmosphere. Mutual respect, trust in their fellows, and the ability to collaborate with other Wiccans are other reasons that many people decide to join a coven. Many covens are also more socially active, as well as more socially pro-active, meaning that as a group, some covens will perform a ritual, either privately or publicly, as not only a statement on the issue being focused on but to raise awareness of their political stance. Other coven members want more of a sense of hierarchy in a coven, with a High Priestess or Priest presiding over rituals, and initiates passing the three degrees, to go on and start their own covens. Still, others want the formal training that being initiated into a Tradition provides, along with the resources of a practicing coven, where all members contribute to the learning aspects of their Wiccan Traditions.

A coven with multiple members can also raise more energies during rituals than a solitary practitioner, and therefore can at times accomplish more. A sense of security in being part of a fixed group, or being able to tackle societal issues that are impossible for one person alone, are other benefits for those looking to join covens. Whatever your reasons for wanting to join a coven, the first thing you'll want to do is think about the reasons you want to join a coven. You may wish to be part of a coven for any of the reasons above or one of your own, just make sure you know why it is for you. Many Wiccans often will meditate on this question, or even perform their own ritual for clarity and insight. Some Wiccans even perform a ritual to ask the Mother to help in finding a coven, this puts the issue into the hands of the Goddess, and She will send you what you need. Check online for local forums that are Pagan or Wiccan oriented. Or find out if there are any Pagan workshops at your closest library or college.

Many who practice The Craft wear some sort of jewelry to symbolize their Wiccan faith. If you make your Intent known to the Universe, it will give you what you need. As people grow in their Wiccan faith and spiritual awareness, they may also "outgrow" their coven, as they experiment with new philosophies and change their ideologies over time. Covens can fall victim to power struggles or internal strife over personal differences, just like any other groups or families. They can often feel too confining for a Wiccan who has forged their path and now has to learn a new set of "rules" to follow. A coven is susceptible of losing its focus, as well, either as a functioning coven, where the meetings are treated more like social functions than rituals or as activists, that concentrate more on the political ramifications, than the actual spirituality of Wicca.

The most important thing to remember, if you are thinking about joining a coven, is to make sure that not only is the coven right for you but that you will fit into the group seamlessly. You'll want to know things like which Tradition do they follow and which Divinities, of course. Ask about their rituals and what Sabbats are most important to them, and their method of casting a circle. Some questions you may include are how often they meet (You don't want to find out after you've joined that the coven meets twice a week when you are working; Whether they are a "closeted" group or not (A Wiccan who is closeted is a practitioner of Wicca, that has been secretive about their Wiccan faith, if you aren't "in the Broom Closet yourself, be careful not to "out" a coven that is, for whatever reason), You may also want to consider whether or not the coven's ideologies and your own agree when it comes to doing a ritual "sky-clad" or not, or you may find yourself in an awkward situation! But don't worry, if they have invited you to be initiated into their coven, they'll be curious about you in turn , this will give both you and your prospective coven a solid understanding of each other, so you can build trust, and respect, which are crucial for the success of a coven. Prospective coven members could even become a spiritual family for you, because, like a family, a coven should add acceptance, love, respect, and guidance to your spiritual journey.

Some Wiccans decide that solitary practice is the best fit for them. A solitary Wiccan is one who has decided to pursue their spiritual choice alone, and there is a myriad of reasons to do so. Many solitaries, as they are called, decide to practice Wicca alone because of the sense of freedom it gives them. You may want to practice alone because you haven't quite nailed down your ritual style, and you don't want anything to influence it. Witches may not join a coven either from philosophical or spiritual views. Many Hedge witches are solitary practitioners because it is simply a solitary Tradition, calling for long hours in Nature, studying all She has to teach you, but not easily practiced in large groups! Even time constraints could otherwise prevent someone from being a part of rituals or gatherings in a coven, and therefore a large part of what a coven does. There may even be geographical factors preventing a solitary Wiccan form joining a coven if you live in an area where there isn't a large Wiccan presence, although these are becoming much more infrequent, with the advent of the internet. You don't have to be in a coven to be a Wiccan practitioner, you only have to live the Wiccan way. Although a sense of freedom from having to fit into a Tradition can be liberating, it also comes with some inherent drawbacks, such as a limit to the power an individual can raise energetically as compared with that of a large coven, or the lack of any spiritual guidance and collective knowledge. Research for the solitary is sometimes a chore when you must start fresh on every subject, with no inroads already in place. These issues can often be overcome with persistence and a bit of determination, but there are still times when the solitary practitioner will end up feeling, well... alone.

Of course, in this electronic age of video blogs, online newsletters and message boards, a solitary practitioner isn't truly alone at all. Many Wiccans are just a keyboard and internet connection away, and most are happy to share knowledge, insight, and companionship. There are even Wiccan and witchcraft correspondence courses you can find online now. There are also Circles to turn to if joining a coven isn't the right choice for you, and you don't want to practice *entirely* alone. A Circle of Wiccans are a group of people who meet more informally than a coven, often not having a fixed membership, they either may or may not have an initiation of new members. Some benefits of this being that there will always be a new insight, and fresh energy to work with, a Circle group will very seldom feel stagnant during rituals with new or returning group members adding energies that weren't there last time they met. Research is dynamic is Circles, because there is such a diverse gathering of witches, each with their own lore and knowledge to share. Because of time constraints, many Wiccans can't commit to the more regular schedule of a coven, so a Circle group that meets more infrequently meets their needs better.

Some Witches prefer more of a loosely structured hierarchy, rather than the more rigid system in a Tradition like Gardnerianism. Or a witch may be between covens and hasn't had time to find one before she Sabbat they want to celebrate. One of the largest benefits of a Circle group is the inclusivity and tolerance of other beliefs and ideas within Wicca. Within one Circle, you may find a practicing Hedgewitch, there to celebrate the Summer Solstice, next to a witch that has just moved from another state and hasn't decided yet whether another coven is right for her. In the same group you might find a mother who practices Celtic Wicca but doesn't want to join a coven because of her two children in soccer playoffs. The general "rule" of a Circle group is acceptance. Gatherings and Circles can have their drawbacks, as well. There are times when a Circle's energies don't work well together or even outright clash. This is often a problem of the Group not coming together to practice often enough to let the members get to know the feel of the other members' energies and the way they work together. There are also times when the number of members available to perform rituals doesn't meet the needs of the ritual itself. This problem can arise if there are no set attendance standards for the Circle. So whether you decide to join a formal coven, practice informally for the Sabbats with a Circle gathering or take your besom and "fly" solo, as you know by now, the only person who can make the right choice for you IS you!

Hopefully, now you have a solid understanding of Wicca, both as spirituality and as a practice. There are so many reasons to choose Wicca as your Faith and the ability to forge your Spiritual Journey is one of the most compelling and rewarding. As you journey, you will learn more, and become more aware of the energetic ways we are connected through Nature and The Goddess that exist in everything, as well as finding out how to coexist with them. Wicca is one of the fastest-growing spiritual paths in our time and has in the incredibly diverse following, each one adding a different nuance and outlook to the Faith as they grow. I hope you will find that Wicca is a vibrant, and fulfilling spirituality made up of a myriad of theologies, ritual and Witchcraft to explore and find Wonder in!

Conclusion

Now that we have explored the elements and ways to establish one's self on the Wiccan path, the key is to explore and experience the magic for yourself. Begin exploring various forms of spells, rituals and observing the magic of life around you. May this book serve as a guide for you along the path, encourage you to understand the divinity of your being. Now you have the skillset and knowledge to connect with the elements, breathe with the seasons and attract onto you all that will bring the greatest peace to yourself. Yet as we have shared and noted, the path is one of experimentation and personal experience. So, take this journey to explore the information and knowledge within this book, see what resonates for you, what allows the deepest connection to your own highest good. Share with other Wiccans along the path to gain deeper knowledge.

Allow your journey to take shape and form in whichever way Spirit may guide you. Try both ways of the Wiccan path, seek a coven within your area, join a circle, join an Esbat or Solstice ceremony if you can. Yet also take the time to venture this path as a solitary Wiccan, notice which path is best suited for you. Dive into exploring if you are a Hedge Witch, a Sea Witch, a Tech Witch, a Kitchen Witch, Gardnerian Witch or Alexandrian Witch, or maybe even a new form of Wiccan Witch altogether, this is your path and your expression of the craft.

Once have connected more truly with the elements, you coven or self, what form of witchcraft calls to you. Begin your journey with spells, rituals and incantations. For some herbalism will be the most potent magic, others candle magic will call to you. You may even find you are a reader of the Tarot. Come back to this book at anytime to rediscover keys terms, spells, or concepts of Wicca as you dive deep into the Craft.

Remember above all *"Bide the Wiccan Laws ye must In Perfect Love and Perfect Trust. Live an' let live - Fairly take an' fairly give."* Know that this knowledge and wisdom has been passed down through tradition and in time, to guide and serve you along the path into your highest good. May you continue to share this wisdom and magic in perfect love and perfect trust. To keep, as was the vision of Scire, the ways of old alive to benefit all beings, elementals and natural order.

Thank you for making it through to the end of Wicca For Beginners: *The ultimate guide to Wiccan magic, traditions, rituals, and deities. How to follow the Witchcraft Path for the solitary practitioner.* I hope you now have a basic understanding of not only witchcraft, but the Wiccan spiritual choice, as well. Now is the time to join in The Craft and lend your energies to the collective of all those who are journeying along with you on your Wiccan Way!

Namaste!

www.ingramcontent.com/pod-product-compliance
Lightning Source LLC
Chambersburg PA
CBHW081420080526
44589CB00016B/2612